AMERICANS
THROUGH THE LENS

AMERICANS
THROUGH THE LENS

SANDRA FORTY

Thunder Bay
P · R · E · S · S

San Diego, California

Th
P
Adv
588
CA
ww

Pro
8–1
Roa
A m
Chr

© 2

Cop
Pan
Cop
All r
No
repr
form
or n
copy
info
syst
sion

Brie
1,00
revi

All r
sion
Thu
edit
abov
All c
inqu
conc
bool
PRO
Blen
Lond
A m
Chry

ISBN

Libra
Publ
requ

Print

1 2

Not for nothing has the United States of America been called the "Land of Opportunity"—for that is exactly what it always has been. For centuries, America has welcomed all sorts of people to its shores—migrants escaping economic adversity in their homelands, adventurers, and religious dissenters, as well as ordinary families—their only desire to find a better life in a new land. Other new Americans arrived unwillingly, notably the African-American slaves and indentured servants, but most immigrants came hoping to improve their lives and provide a better future for themselves and their families.

From the earliest days of photography, life in America as experienced by Americans—both old and new—has been chronicled. Sometimes these chronicles take the form of intimate family records; more often, as with the photographs shown in this book, photographs were taken for publication in magazines and newspapers, which in turn sent pictures of America across the continent and around the world. Most of these photographs were taken by professional photographers as a record of Americans going about their daily lives as they saw them through their lenses. These are not personal family photos, but rather pictures taken to depict and explain the ways of life of the more and more diverse American peoples to an audience far beyond the strict locality of the picture.

America as a vastly diverse land of different peoples is familiar through television and movies, but photographs such as the ones in this book set the time and place forever, bringing to bear a focus and intensity that no other medium possesses. Many of the photographs are fascinating for the insight they present of a world in the past that has disappeared forever as technology has superseded the old and replaced it with the new, often obliterating all traces of the former.

Since the mid-nineteenth century, America has been a world leader in technology and science, and consequently Americans have enjoyed the considerable advantages that such new developments have brought. Although the Industrial Revolution originated in Great Britain, American businessmen were quick to follow up and then overtake the rest of the world with the latest inventions. Technologies such as the telegraph, steam-driven machinery, electricity, building and construction technologies, and the internal combustion engine were all developed in America. All had a radical effect on the daily lives of Americans. In the early 1900s the biggest change in transportation, and

Left: Photographer Matthew Brady (1823–1896), in top hat, stands next to General Samuel P. Heintzelman on the steps of the former Lee mansion in Arlington, Virginia in 1862, along with members of the General's staff. In spite of his acclaimed photographs of the Civil War, Brady died in poverty in a New York almshouse.

therefore in day-to-day living, was the exchange of the horse for the motorcar, while in the closing decades of the century one of the greatest revolutions was the replacement of the typewriter with the computer. Such spectacular revolutions completely revise how people live and work, and without photographs it is only too easy to forget just how big a change such technological innovations have made.

The photographs in this book show Americans as seen through the lenses of many photographers. They show the country and her inhabitants in all their great diversity. Many are spontaneous pictures catching a moment in time that speaks for itself, such as the awful conflagration of the *Hindenburg*; others are carefully posed to present a particular impression of an event or a person. These latter pictures, although arguably artificial, show how the subjects wished to present themselves to the world and how they wanted to be accepted, as perfection itself with no weaknesses or flaws.

The earliest ventures into photography using light-sensitive paper and chemicals to reproduce an image were developed first in France in 1839, then in England. Many inventors turned their minds to the development of photography and advances in the field were rapid as well as eagerly awaited by a photo-hungry public. The still-cumbersome technology was brought to these shores by some of the earliest photographers as well as by wealthy Americans who toyed enthusiastically with the new invention. The earliest recognizable photographs of people were all studio-based endeavors using large format cameras and, in effect, still-life subjects. This was because the sitter had to hold still, sometimes for minutes at a time, which explains the curiously immobile expressions early portraits convey. Many of these same early photos are formal studies of dignitaries and their families who used the new medium of photography to record their importance in a way previously done (at much greater length and expense) by the portrait painter.

Soon the more adventurous photographers took their cameras and paraphernalia outside and began to record the world around them. The bravest took their equipment out into the wild lands to photograph America as she developed and in the process recorded a dying culture being rapidly overrun by technology. In the mid-nineteenth century, the pace of life was much slower and seemingly unchanging, but technological changes brought about by the Industrial Revolution inexorably worked their way into the lives of Americans even in the farthest reaches of the land. These photographers struggled with heavy,

Left: The self-portrait of Robert Cornelius (1809–1893), the very first daguerreotype taken in North America, c. 1839.

Right: U.S. frontierswoman Calamity Jane (Martha Jane Burk, 1852–1903), celebrated for her bravery and her skill in riding and shooting during the gold rush days in Dakota, c. 1882.

cumbersome equipment, which makes the wonderful photos they produced all the more amazing. The earliest negatives were taken on large, fragile glass plates, many of which did not survive the journey to the processing laboratory. That any of these plates survived at all is as remarkable as the pictures they produced.

These earliest photographs are in many ways the most fascinating records of all, as they show a largely preindustrial America where the horse and cart were the prime methods of transportation, communication, and an outward sign of wealth. They show a period long lost to living memory and only available otherwise from written sources such as journals and newspaper reports. Some of the most remarkable photographs of all depict the soldiers and battlefields of the Civil War, a period so far away as to be classified as history, but brought to life by photographs in a way that no other records can achieve.

Other photos show how America, as we've come to know it, was grappled and bullied out of the virgin soil by single-minded, driven pioneers and settlers, and forced into cultivation. The pictures of their sparse but proud homesteads are a lesson in endurance—they suffered through hard times but saw it through to build America as it is today. The photos go on to show how the modest settlements grew into small towns, then into cities, and finally into vast urban conurbations where each individual town merges seamlessly into another.

The great revolution in photography happened in 1884 when former bank clerk and New Yorker George Eastman invented flexible paper roll film. He followed that with the Kodak camera in 1888; this was a hand-held box which used the new roll film. In a stroke, cameras became portable, lightweight, inexpensive, and therefore increasingly accessible to would-be photographers.

To cover a subject as vast as America, this book has been split into distinct sections exploring the main aspects of Americans going about their lives. The first part, *American People*, looks at the many and various peoples who came together to become Americans—starting with the Native Americans recorded as they looked and lived in the days before their centuries-old lifestyle was swept away in the name of progress. Something of the harsh conditions that the pioneers encountered is apparent in their photos, as are the difficulties faced by the settlers. All of them arrived in America to build new lives for themselves—although for many, it was sheer determination that led to success. Other early settlers came against their will, namely the African-American slaves brought to these shores for cheap labor. Their plight was not extensively recorded—it was not a situation that their owners wanted unduly publicized. The section finishes with the most optimistic and ambitious of immigrants, the gold prospectors, ever hopeful of a fortune glittering in the next shovelful of soil.

Left: Alice Cunningham Fletcher (1838–1923), a pioneer in the study of Native Americans, making a record of Native American music in 1895.

Right: Visitors viewing the Plymouth Rock in 1950. The rock was enshrined in a Grecian Temple by the Colonial Dames in 1920 and is supposed to pinpoint where the first American settlers landed.

Americans have always loved a good political dustup and the next part, *Americans in Politics*, starts with the presidents, many of whom are seen here as they were before the mantle of power elevated them above their peers. The awful years of the Great Depression show the utter devastation in human lives brought about by the turbulence of the stock market. The forces of law and order that comprised the long arm of the law are pictured, along with some of their greatest protagonists. Next, we see images of the vast numbers involved in the civil rights struggles for equality and freedom. The last section looks at that over-romanticized period, Prohibition, and how it was enforced and circumvented.

The third part, *Americans at War*, looks at the major conflicts in which America has been involved, all the way from the Civil War and the Spanish-American War through the tragedy of the great World Wars, and finally to two conflicts in the Far East, Korea and Vietnam. In the case of Vietnam, we witness the awful pall that the war cast over the nation.

Part Four, *Building America*, shows how this country changed from a largely rural, agricultural society to a modern industrialized nation at the forefront of world technology with communications stretching from coast to coast. Early photographs show how the infrastructure was assembled through the building of roads, bridges, and canals. We see how the towns developed into cities and how the great transcontinental railroads were built. Then finally, the ultimate journey into space with the Apollo moon program.

Part Five comes down to the personal level and looks at how Americans actually lived—in the country and in the cities. Public, then private transportation changed the way everyone lived. Within the space of a few short years an American could get into an automobile and drive across the country in a few days to look for work on the other seaboard. This was previously unimaginable for all but the very richest people. Another important aspect of daily life is religion, and in America, thanks to broadly tolerant laws, there are a wide variety of faiths practiced by otherwise ordinary Americans.

In *America at Work*, the photographs show how technology changed the workplace and how women moved out of the home into jobs and careers. Feminist politics came to the fore with the temperance movement and developed into the suffragette movement with women demanding equal rights. The final part, *Americans at Play*, looks at how Americans use their leisure time and enjoy themselves.

Photography itself is constantly changing. Now that so much of it is digital and computer-generated, there is less use for still photography as a means of informing people how the world is working. Most of the images we receive are incessantly moving, barely focusing on one subject before moving on to the next. The golden age of the photograph lasted just over a hundred years from the wonder of its earliest days in the 1870s until the 1970s, when moving images replaced photographs as the prime method of visual information. This book is a celebration of that golden age.

Left: Just moments before John F. Kennedy, the 35th president of the United States, was assassinated, the presidential motorcade drives through Dallas.

Far Left: A full-length outdoor group portrait of the Cannonball Motorcycle Messengers and the Parcel Delivery Service. Seven messengers sit on their motorbikes in front of this store in 1910.

NATIVE AMERICANS

The forefathers of the Native Americans settled the North and South American continents in a series of migrations across the Bering Strait from as early as 40,000 years ago. They became hunter-gatherer inhabitants of the woods, coasts, mountains, prairies, and deserts of America. Native Americans lived for thousands of years undisturbed by any but their own kind until European explorers and settlers arrived. Initially, both sides viewed each other with curiosity rather than hostility, but this situation rapidly changed as the newcomers started to covet and then openly acquire native lands. Worse still, after contact with European settlers, many Native Americans suffered terribly from cholera and smallpox, and their populations were decimated by Western diseases and illnesses.

At the time the Europeans arrived, there were numerous Native American tribes scattered across the country from coast to coast and from the Arctic to the Caribbean. Many of these groupings were nomadic, ranging over large distances. There was a rich cultural and territorial diversity that produced many different languages—about fifty-five different tongues plus many further dialect variations—customs, dress, and beliefs.

When the Europeans arrived, the Native Americans were living in close and harmonious association with the land. Their culture was one of sharing—they shared their meager possessions, food, and above all, the land. On tribal lands, a man was free to build his tepee or lodge anywhere and cultivate the ground around with corn. Land would become a matter of particular issue in the years that followed. Native Americans could not understand the settlers' greed for more land than they personally needed to house and feed their families. Furthermore, because of their apparently simple—in many

Previous Page: Native Americans in traditional Plains dress, c. 1900, with their tents pitched in open country. Their horse pulls a travois, a sled-like implement made up from two poles joined by a bracing frame.

Right: Chief of the Chiricahua Apache, Geronimo (1829-1909) is at far right in this 1886 photograph. The Apaches were the last tribe to surrender to the American government when Geronimo gave himself up to General Crook in Sonora, Mexico in 1886. His tribe was sent first to Florida, then Alabama, and finally to Fort Sill, Oklahoma in 1894. In 1913, just over two-thirds of the remaining (187) Chiricahua returned to their traditional hunting grounds and settled on the Mescalero Reservation in New Mexico. They had originally lived on the west side of the Rio Grande in Arizona, Mexico, and New Mexico—land actively sought after by first Spanish and then American ranchers, settlers, and miners in some of the most bitter of all Native American territorial disputes.

Above: A Pawnee family poses outside their earth lodge at Loup, Nebraska, c. 1871. Pawnee lands in Nebraska were almost all lost through treaties with the U.S. government, the only exception being a single reservation in what is now Nance County. The majority of the tribe moved to lands adjoining the Arkansas River. Although the Pawnees were mainly nomadic and lived in tepees, they were farmers who grew corn, beans, squash, and pumpkins, supplementing this diet with buffalo and other types of game.

Right: Wrapped in blankets, a family of Menominee outside a traditional lodge, c. 1900. They belong to the Alonquian tribes, originally of the Eastern Woodlands culture, around Wisconsin. Menominee lived as hunter-gatherers along the Menominee River.

Far Right: "Digger" Indians, members of the southern branch of the Paiute tribe camped near Mendocino in 1876. They lived around southern Utah, Nevada, and in Arizona above the Colorado River. Paiute lived an itinerant life in wickiups—huts of stick and brush fastened to poles made from willow trees—catching and eating small game and supplementing their diet with any fruits, nuts, and vegetables they could find.

cases hunter-gathering—lifestyle, Native Americans were held in contempt by the settlers and considered inferior; their very closeness with the land was considered proof of this. They were seen as no more than savage hunters, even those who farmed, such as the Iroquois and Cherokee. This was a convenient excuse used to justify the taking of their lands.

After the American Revolution established the new nation, the native position became more perilous. Previously they could play off the British against the French; now they had the United States government to deal with. To reassure natives of the security of their position, the U.S. President became the "Great Father of the Indians," but most incumbents did little, if anything, to protect their charges from rapacious land-grabbers. For example, under the Indian Removal Act of 1830, the 60,000 people of the Five Civilized Tribes were removed summarily from their traditional lands. Any perceived legal violation by the tribes brought horrendous and totally inproportionate reprisals.

The settlers wanted more and more of the native lands and used any and all means to acquire them. Native chieftains were coerced into becoming cosignatories to treaties which guaranteed them lands in the far west, lands which were removed from them again within a short span of years. Many thousands (particularly children and elders) died on the long, enforced cross-country journeys to the new lands, or at the holding stations into which they were corralled along the way.

The new settlers needed their acquisition of native land to have the trappings of legality, so their claims could stand scrutiny in court. Many subterfuges were used to achieve this—bribery was used to tempt tribal chiefs to part with tribal lands, and it was not unusual that a mere fragment of the tribe was considered empowered to speak for an entire people when it came to the surrender of lands. Another method was to find an amenable native who could be dubbed tribal chief for legal purposes and therefore be placed in a position of power to hand over the land.

The Removal Act of 1830 and the Allotment Act of 1887 gave a legal facade to the appropriation of the land. The latter—by general connivance of Congress—passed supposedly to benefit the Native Americans, not to exploit them. By this Act they lost seventeen million acres, one-seventh of their remaining lands. Between 1887 and 1934, Native Americans lost eighty-six million acres of valuable land and received in exchange smaller quantities of poorer and less agriculturally viable ground.

By the 1920s, the Native Americans were in such disarray that many tribes were on the verge of famine, living on land that could not sustain their needs. However, things began to change at the end of this decade. Presidents Hoover and Roosevelt took steps that would see agricultural productivity increase, populations soar, and improvement in business, education, and tribal self-government. A long fight for justice and recompense started, but it would take many years of struggle to achieve anything. Increased militancy—including lawsuits for compensation and even armed confrontation, as at Wounded Knee in 1973—led to the Indian Self-determination Act of 1975, when a more enlightened Congress promoted the policy of tribal restoration. Today, Native Americans have reestablished their identity to a level that seemed impossible at the end of the nineteenth century.

Above left: A Native American youth, with the Anglicized name of "Shows As He Goes," c. 1907.

Above: The painted face of Moshe, a young Mohave girl, from 1903. The Mohave lived in lands that are now in Nevada, Arizona, and California. They were a desert Yuman tribe who subsisted off plants and a little fishing and hunting when the seasons permitted. They were given land at Fort Mohave and the Colorado River Indian reservations.

Right: Bird Rattle, who was probably a Spokane tribesman from Washington, seen in 1910. These Native Americans originate around the Spokane and Little Spokane Rivers in eastern Washington. When their lands were taken, most went to the Spokane Reservation at Wellpinit, Washington, while a few joined the Flatheads in Montana.

Left: A Navajo silversmith with a conch belt, c. 1885. His tools are displayed on their carrying pouch. The Navajo come from the dry deserts of north Arizona and northwestern New Mexico. They domesticated sheep and horses, and took on many Spanish and Pueblo Indian influences. Navajo are famed for their fine silverwork and textile work with woolen rugs and blankets.

Above: An Inuit carpenter at work using a traditional bow drill which he holds with his mouth and turns with a string, c. 1910. Inuit means "raw meat eaters," and is a term that has been applied to the Native American tribes which live in the cold northern reaches of the country.

Right: Native Americans performing the Taos Eagle Dance at the Gallup Ceremonials in New Mexico, c. 1955. Gatherings of the tribes are important and colorful ceremonial occasions.

Above: The Seminole tribe of Native Americans in Florida have a tradition of wrestling alligators, the secret techniques for which have been passed on from one generation to the next. The picture shows five men who have just passed the final test at an alligator wrestling school in Musa Isle Village, near Miami, Florida, in 1962. Many Seminole were moved to Indian Territory (now Oklahoma) but a few remained in the remote southern swamps of Florida. Their distinctive clothing consists of colorful quilted clothes.

Right: Eighty-year-old Mrs. Johnny Bear had knitted Cowichan sweaters for half a century when this photograph was taken on June 8, 1964. Behind her stands the now-deserted stone church where the first group of Cowichan women knitted together.

Far Right: Native American Seminole chief Willie Osoeola, balancing on his dugout canoe, takes aim with his crab-like pincers at an unsuspecting frog in this c. 1941 photograph. He sold frogs' legs to hotels and restaurants for a living.

SETTLERS

Settlers, as the term suggests, were the people who came to the United States to stay, who wanted to put down roots and grow with the land. The term refers principally to people who settled on the Great Plains. They were invariably hard-working people, sometimes farming families from Europe forced off their ancestral lands by high rents and crippling agricultural famines; but most were Americans from the Eastern states who were looking for a better future. What they got was a hard life, breaking new ground to grow crops and forging new townships out of hostile territory. They were brave, single-minded people who had chosen their lot in life and were determined to make good. Such a vast land as America had, in the early days of settlement and exploration, wide open spaces enough for all who cared to stake a claim, to such an extent that the government actually gave away land until 1890 when the frontier was closed.

Already by the 1830s almost all of the rich Midwestern land was claimed and settled, and the fertile Southern lands had all but disappeared into vast plantations. The next area for expansion was the Great Plains of Missouri and Arkansas—the far West was too remote and still too dangerous. This changed in the 1840s, when trails were established through the Rockies. Pioneers undertook the hazardous journey in large numbers, using the Oregon, Santa Fe, and California trails into California and Oregon Territory. Between 1841 and 1867, an estimated 350,000 settlers migrated to the West. In addition, another type of settler came to stay—the Mormons, who grew in numbers in Utah. They worked as cooperative farmers and through their religion were able to bring a rare stability to the frontier; by 1870, there were 87,000 Mormons in Utah.

Various acts were passed to legislate land acquisition. The first was the Homestead Act of 1862, granting 160 acres of public land to any citizen who occupied it for five years. The Desert Land Act of 1877 allowed a settler to buy up to 640 acres for a filing fee of $1.25, on condition that he irrigated the land within two years. The following year the Timber and Stone Act allowed the purchase of land for the

Right: A family poses with their wagon in Loup Valley, Nebraska, on their way to a new homestead in 1886. The Homestead Act of 1862 allowed any citizen over the age of twenty-one to claim 160 acres of public land for the price of a filing fee, provided they improved the land and resided there for five years. In fact, relatively few homesteaders did acquire land under the act; a total of eighty million acres (a mere drop in the ocean) was awarded between 600,000 claimants between 1862 and 1900, but many of these people were frauds acting as cover for big business concerns who were anxious to acquire as much free land as they could get away with.

exploitation of timber and stone at $2.50 an acre, on up to 160 acres of land deemed unsuitable for agriculture. But rather than benefiting the small farmer, these acts helped rapacious ranchers and timber merchants to grab and exploit the land—the very groups the acts were designed to exclude—by putting up false claimants for the grants.

Far more successful in attracting settlers were the inducements offered by the new railroads, which were looking to increase rail traffic and sell off the excess lands adjoining their tracks. Unable to get sufficient takers at home, the rail and road companies sent immigration agents to Europe offering fertile farmland (usually it wasn't) and well-paid jobs (usually they weren't) to new settlers, and even offered assisted transatlantic passage to prospective settlers.

Times were hard for the settlers. Even if they got the 160 acres free (except for the administration charge), they needed money to build their homes, for agricultural tools, livestock, seed to grow crops, and machinery for harvesting, transportation, and storage. Furthermore, because of the vast differences in land quality, climate, and terrain, the land grants in some areas were just too small to provide a living. However, one big problem faced by the new settler—that of securing his farm boundary—was solved in 1874 when Joseph F. Giddon, an Illinois farmer, put his new invention, barbed wire, on the market. This cheap and simple expedient became an instant success and within six years much of the Plains were enclosed.

In spite of all the privations—isolation, dangerous wildlife, mosquitoes, tornadoes, and extreme climate, to mention but a few—life on the Plains was an attractive prospect for those people who otherwise had nothing. The population in Nebraska, Kansas, Iowa, Minnesota, and the Dakotas, which stood at one million in 1860, had leapt to over seven million by the turn of the century.

Although the pioneers led an isolated existence, they soon established the cultural institutions of the West, such as newspapers, schools, and law enforcement. This process increased as more and more women joined their menfolk and new families started to grow. But life was still hard, and as their sons and daughters grew up, they started to drift back to the towns and cities to earn an easier living. Mechanization meant fewer jobs on the land while at the same time industrialization created more jobs in the factories and cities of America.

Above Right: An 1871 photograph showing a land office in a California town, for the buying and selling of land. A sign next door advertises the depot for the Mechanics' Institute Fair.

Right: A family outside their home on the Plains, c. 1885. Drought was a constant threat for such families, and very few farms had the luxury of a nearby water supply. This was solved in part by the digging of very deep wells to tap into the sub-surface strata, the water being brought to the surface by steel windmills specially designed to cope with the conditions on the Plains.

Above: An ex-slave family outside their house in Nebraska in 1888. Many freed slaves moved to the Plains in the decades after the American Civil War.

Left: Judge Henry H. Campbell standing outside a cabin on the Matador Ranch in Texas, in 1908. Conditions out on the Plains were harsh and only the toughest thrived. Settlers had to be self-reliant in every way as the nearest neighbor could be miles away and the civilization of a township even further.

Right: An African-American family outside a shack in Oklahoma, 1901. After the end of the Civil War the Homestead Act was modified to grant 46 million acres of federal land in the South. Congress intended the act to benefit the freed slaves, but much of the land was far too poor and unsuited to agriculture for a family to survive on.

Far Left, Top: A Forest Service Ranger outside his log cabin in the Wallowa National Forest, Oregon, c. 1908. The majority of the new settlers in the West were men: in Colorado in 1880, men outnumbered women two to one, while in Wyoming the ratio was closer to three to one.

Far Left, Bottom: Trappers at Brown's Basin in Arizona, 1908

Left: A Russian Orthodox church built by a colony of fifty White Russians, formerly loyal to the Czar, near Lakewood, New Jersey, c. 1937. The immigrants were helped by the New Deal's Rural Rehabilitation Project. Settlers generally were quick to establish churches as they provided a focus for the local community and a source of strength in difficult times.

SLAVERY

The first record of Africans arriving as slaves in America is in 1619. The trade slowly picked up, until by the eighteenth century an average of 3,000 Africans arrived each month. By the second half of that century, at least one-fifth of the population of America was of African origin. Slavery had become hereditary by the turn of the eighteenth century and had the status (although far less importance) of property. They worked on the large tobacco and rice plantations in Virginia and Maryland, but this decreased by the early 1800s. The real importance of slaves was in the increasingly profitable business of growing cotton in the deep South. Initially, cotton could only be grown in the coastal regions of Georgia and South Carolina, but the industry was revolutionized in 1793 when Eli Whitney invented the cotton gin, a machine which could sort the seed even from short fibers (which inland cotton plants produced). This meant that cotton could be grown as a viable crop in the rich soils of Alabama, Mississippi, and even into Texas. Slaves were far and away the cheapest form of labor.

By 1850, about six million whites lived in the South, and of these, 347,000 owned slaves; about half that number owned fewer than five slaves each. The largest concentrations of slaves were workers on the plantations. By 1860, the slave population—many of them cotton workers—was just under four million.

By the start of the nineteenth century, Abolitionists—led in many cases by religious groups such as the Quakers—were becoming more vocal about the plight of slaves, but public support was slow to accumulate, even in the industrialized North. Broadly speaking, the Southern states wanted the retention of slavery, and the Northern states wanted its repeal. After long arguments, the Missouri Compromise was reached in 1820 and America was partitioned by a line drawn at parallel 36° 30' north. North of this line any future states would not allow slavery, while to the south slavery was permitted. The largely open West was still technically slave-free, but when California was granted statehood, it joined the territories of Utah and New Mexico as being able to choose whether to be slave

Right: A group of escaped slaves outside a cabin in 1861. Escaped slaves were known as contrabands after the Union General Benjamin Butler (1818–1893) announced that any slaves in land controlled by the Union Army would be regarded as contraband property.

Left: A slave family in South Carolina, 1862.

Below: Ex-slave, Abolitionist, agent of the Massachusetts Anti-Slavery Society, and U.S.S Minister to Haiti in 1889, Frederick Douglass (1817-1895) pictured c. 1855. *Narrative*, his harrowing personal story of enslavement and ultimate escape in Maryland, was widely read and awoke Northerners to the true horrors of slavery. He also founded the first successful black newspaper, *North Star*, in 1847.

Right: The horrifically scarred back of a slave after whipping, 1863.

Far Right: A shirtless slave stands with his hands tied to a whipping post waiting for the beating, c. 1865. Note the stocks built on top of the whipping post.

Below Right: Black workers planting sweet potatoes, Edisto Island, North Carolina, 1862.

holding or not, to keep the compromise balance of free and slave states even.

A constant complaint from Southern landlords was that the Northern justiciary would not capture and return escaped slaves. A new law was passed, the Fugitive State Law, whereby an accused escapee was tried before a federal commissioner to prove his status. At the same time, all American citizens were forbidden to assist, rescue, or aid an escaped slave. This last act resulted in open riot on a number of occasions in the North when angry crowds intervened to prevent the capture of fleeing slaves.

The issue of slavery was at the heart of the American Civil War, with the "free" Union North against the slaveholding South. The Union finally prevailed and on January 1, 1863, President Lincoln passed the Emancipation Proclamation, legally freeing all the slaves in the South. The Civil War Amendments to the Constitution after the Union victory in the Civil War abolished slavery in the United States. Citizenship was granted automatically to all former slaves and all the men were given the right to vote.

The obvious benefits of emancipation, however, could not hide the difficulties. Suddenly, large numbers of former slaves were left to fend for themselves with little or no resources. Few had received any education and still fewer had any land from which to make a living. With no better alternative, many former slaves became sharecroppers, working long, hard hours to pay back rents and loans to their former masters. The legacy of slavery was a bitter one that continues to haunt the country to the present day.

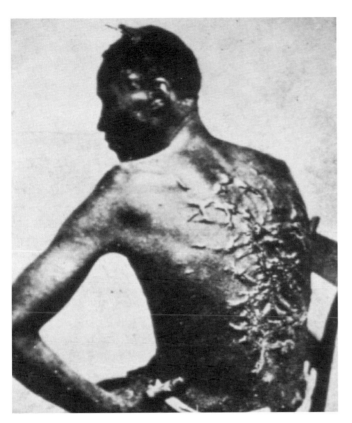

Above: A group of former slaves on a riverfront dock in Virginia. 1865. Not all slaves had worked on the land. Many were servants and many more were skilled craftsmen—such as carpenters, coopers, masons, and bricklayers. They also worked in mines and factories, in lumber yards, foundries, and on the steamboats.

Left: A school for freed slaves, 1870. Many former slaves lacked any form of education and were consequently at a disadvantage compared to equally poor, but white, workers. Such schools provided an invaluable service.

Right: A c. 1930 photograph of a former slave standing by the slave block in Fredericksburg, Virginia, on which slaves stood to be auctioned off to the highest bidder. At such auctions men and women were separated never to see each other again, and even more heartbreaking, mothers and children were parted. Slaves could be married but the ceremony carried no force of law and the bond could be broken at the owner's whim. Plantation owners did not usually split families unnecessarily because it was bad for the workers' morale. However, sometimes an owner needed to raise money and selling slaves was an easy answer. A slave was a planter's most valuable asset; just before the Civil War a healthy young male slave could be worth $1,800. The internal slave trade just prior to the opening of the Civil War is estimated to have been worth $60 million and involved about 80,000 slaves.

Left: On the far left of this photograph, taken in about 1900, is legendary Abolitionist leader Harriet Tubman (c. 1820–1913), escaped slave and founder of the "Underground Railroad," which provided safe houses for escaping slaves on their way to freedom in the North and in Canada. The Underground Railroad was not as organized as the mythology has it, but rather a loose and largely spontaneous system of help and shelter for escaped slaves fleeing north to freedom in the years between 1830 and 1860. The number of slaves helped to freedom is uncertain, but many thousands did escape by this means—although this was only a tiny drop in the ocean of millions of slaves. The Underground Railroad route went northwest through Ohio and Indiana or east to New York and New England. It was funded by concerned philanthropists who did what they could to raise funds and goods. The railroad was so called because it used the terminology of the real railroad: it had "conductors," "passengers," and "stations." Harriet Tubman earned the sobriquet "the Moses of her people," by making possibly as many as nineteen perilous journeys to the South to rescue and guide over 200 slaves to freedom in the North. She was so successful that Southern slaveowners put a price of $40,000 on her head—dead or alive.

IMMIGRANTS

The "New World" has been a magnet since the seventeenth century to those whose lives were being ruined by poverty, discrimination, or famine at home—and home could be anywhere in the world. Immigrants have flocked to our shores from all over Europe, Asia, and South America. There were no restrictions on entry to the United States until 1875 when, as an adjunct to an act dealing with contract workers, the government asked local port authorities to count the numbers of immigants. Even then, immigrants could become citizens after five years. Overcrowding in the cities, rampant disease, the rising crime rate, and public unease finally provoked Congress to pass laws to regulate immigration. In 1892, the Ellis Island Immigration Center opened to screen, assess, and ultimately accept or reject applicants for citizenship. Other centers opened simultaneously at other major ports including Boston, Philadelphia, and San Francisco.

Between 1875 and 1917 a number of restrictive immigration laws were passed to disbar complete categories of people, including anyone with a criminal record, prostitutes, lunatics, anyone who needed public charity, political activists, polygamists, illiterates, those with disease, as well as Japanese and Chinese immigrants. Complete immigration control on every category of aspiring citizen was passed in 1921 when Congress set a quota of 358,000 Europeans per year. Of these new citizens, less than a quarter found jobs working on the land; most preferred to stay in the rapidly growing cities of the Northeast and the industrial Midwest.

National origin quotas were also set at three percent of each nation as recorded in the federal census of 1910. This was changed for the National Origins Quota Act in 1924 after strong complaint (because it favored the southern and eastern Europeans too heavily) to two percent of each nationality as shown in the 1890 census, i.e. before the more vilified immigrants arrived in numbers. The Quota Act did indeed stop the southern and eastern Europeans from arriving in numbers, but by then the northern and western Europeans did not apply in sufficient numbers to fill their quotas. However, nonquota countries filled the void and millions of Mexicans, Canadians, West Indians, Filipinos, and Puerto Ricans arrived in the US between 1929 and 1965.

Right: An immigrant family in a tenement slum in New York, c. 1890. Most immigrants arrived in America with sufficient money to travel to find work or to join up with friends and family already settled In towns and cities across America. However, many of the Irish escaping the potato famines in the 1850s and 1880s were so poor that they simply stayed in the environs of New York.

Overall the most numerous immigrants were Germans, followed by Irish, British, and Scandinavians. Smaller but still substantial numbers came from China, the Netherlands, France, Switzerland, and central Europe. In general, the first waves of immigrants up to the late nineteenth century were predominantly from northern and western Europe. The British and Scandinavians assimilated into American society very easily and encountered very little hostility. The Irish, on the other hand, met a lot of opposition and were vilified as lazy, shiftless, and drunken, whereas actually most of them were simply abjectly poor and unemployed.

After about 1890, the tide turned to immigrants predominantly from southern and eastern Europe. They had a harder time fitting into American society as almost none of them spoke English on arrival and furthermore, they looked different, worshipped differently, and dressed exotically.

In the early days there was plenty of paid work to be had in building the new country's roads, rails, and cities, or down in the mines or in the vast forests. There was plenty of work in the factories and burgeoning heavy industries, but because of mechanization, much of the work was unskilled and poorly paid. Only one-fifth of immigrants after 1890 found work on the land.

The cheap price of passage across the Atlantic meant that many immigrants did not come to America to live, but rather to make sufficient money to take home to buy land or start a business. Such people were called "sojourners." They were likely to be young and single, and moved around the country freely as work and whim took them. Some stayed on in the New World, but many others went back to Europe.

Far Left: An 1895 view of Ellis Island in New York Bay. Run by the U.S. Immigration Service. Between 1892 and 1954 over twenty million immigrants passed through on their way to a new life.

Below Left: Immigrants on the deck of the Red Star liner *Westernland*, sailing from Antwerp to New York City in 1901.

Left: Newly arrived Italian immigrants on Ellis Island in 1905.

Below: Passengers and crew on board the immigrant ship SS *Gallia*, bound for the New World. The photograph was taken on July 22, 1895, near Queenstown on the coast of Ireland.

Above: New immigrants being inspected for signs of disease as they arrive in the United States, c. 1900.

Left: Ready for a new life as Americans, an Italian family on board a ferry at the docks to Ellis Island, having successfully cleared through all the immigration tests at the Center, c. 1905.

Right: A young immigrant girl on Ellis Island in 1905.

Above: A customs official attaches labels to the coats of a German immigrant family at the Registry Hall on Ellis Island in 1905.

Left: A mother with her children in a camp for migrant laborers in Nipomo, California, February 1936.

Above Right: Immigrants in a dining hall on Ellis Island in August 1923.

Right: A group of Slav immigrants boarding with a tenement family in New York City. 1912.

Above: Jewish immigrants at Ellis Island with the skyscrapers of New York in the background, c. 1920.

Right: Asian immigrants trying on new clothing, c. 1945. Chinese had arrived in America (in smaller numbers than the European immigrants) principally at San Francisco to work in the mines and on the railroads. They met a considerable amount of hostility from nationalist movements and labor organizations, who feared they would take all their jobs at lower wages. The Chinese Exclusion Act of 1882, was the first such legislation to end Chinese immigration. At this time there were some 105,000 Chinese in the United States, mostly living in California. Their population rapidly fell as they were predominantly male, and those who had families in China were not allowed to bring them to America. This exclusion continued until 1943.

Overleaf: Another sort of immigrant: three British G.I. brides, with their babies in lifejackets, crossing the Atlantic in 1946 to be with their new husbands in a new country. Inevitably, during the war in Europe, young American boys met and fell in love with European, and mainly British, girls.

Left: A family of immigrants gazes at New York's skyline with mixed emotions. They are only three of the 30,000 people who were covered by blanket assurances of the CWS for eventual entry and citizenship. c.1950

Below Left: Two illegal immigrants from Mexico working on a farm tying mustard greens into bunches. 1948.

Right: President Lyndon Baines Johnson (1908–1973) speaking at Ellis Isalnd after he signed the new Immigration Bill at the foot of the Statue of Liberty. New York's skyline is behind him. October 5, 1965.

GOLD RUSH

It started in 1849 in California, with the first and most famous gold rush, and would happen again and again around the world. Thousands of ambitious young men and their followers moved into the largely empty lands west of the Rockies, all anxious to make their fortune by any means available, legal or illegal. In due course the gold rushes flooded the market with such immense quantities of gold that it affected the economy of the United States. Although not actually on the Gold Standard, the U.S. regulated gold against silver at a ratio of sixteen to one, so when the value of gold dropped, the balance of the economy was jeopardized.

The next big strike came in Colorado in 1858-59, then Idaho in 1861-64, Montana in 1863, South Dakota in 1875, and finally Alaska in 1896. At the merest hint of a rumor of a strike, prospectors scrambled to be among the first to lay a new claim. Many prospectors were new immigrants who crossed the Atlantic from their homelands in the hope of striking it rich. Many tried, but few succeeded.

In 1858 when gold was discovered in the Colorado Rockies, an estimated 50,000 miners arrived there within the year. But the gold quickly ran out and many miners moved on to the new strikes around Denver before turning to the silver strikes around Leadville in the early 1870s.

With the opening up of the West and more people prospecting for that elusive fortune, an increasing number of precious mineral strikes were made, with none bigger than the Comstock Lode found in the Washoe district of west Nevada in the late 1850s; in twenty years the gold and silver discovered there amounted to $350 million. Such an enormous find brought thousands of hopeful prospectors flooding to little Virginia City, which quickly turned into a thriving boom town full of bars, banks, and brothels. Mining towns by this time were a byword for lawlessness, disorder, and debauchery.

Right: Spriggs, Lamb, and Dillon—three prospectors panning for gold at Rockerville, South Dakota, in 1889. Over $300,000 of gold was found here between 1876 and 1878. To pan gold, gravel from a suitable outwash (stream or river) is shoveled into a large wash-pan and swished around so that the heavy gold grains fall to the bottom of the pan where they can be extracted. This was hard, tedious work in often freezing water and rarely rewarding enough to scrape much more than a living. But sometimes, the prospector got lucky, and found a gold nugget sufficient to make it all worthwhile.

2357. "We have It Rich." - Washin
panning gold, Rockerville. Dak.
Old-timers, Spriggs, Lamb and Dillor
Photo and copyright by Grabill

and
at work.
1889.

Above: The Gold Hill mining camp in California in 1867. Shanty towns quickly sprang up around the mining areas as tradesmen and women rushed in to provide entertainment and services for the miners. Many Western townships sprang from such inauspicious beginnings as they continued to thrive with other businesses long after the prospectors had moved on to the next claim.

Above Left: Glanville's claim, a California gold mine, c. 1846.

Left: Gold miners washing ore in the Yukon, c. 1900. The Klondike was the last great gold rush in 1896. Some 30,000 people came to this inhospitable region within a few short years, but unlike earlier rushes, many prospectors returned home rather than settling in the region.

Right: A line of gold miners climbing a mountain using a rope during the Klondike gold rush. One of the men is carrying a canoe on his back. Prospectors were notorious for moving around from claim to claim at the slightest rumor of a strike.

Smaller discoveries were made in Idaho and Montana, and some smaller still on the southern edge of the Arizona desert. The last big American gold rush started in 1874 when gold was found in the Black Hills of Dakota. This was deep in Sioux territory and forbidden to intruders, but the army was powerless to stop 15,000 excited prospectors from settling in the area. The tiny town of Deadwood rapidly became one of the most notorious and dangerous places on the entire continent—rivaled only by Tombstone, Arizona—as a result of the Lucky Cross silver find.

However, the outright anarchy of early boom-time days was soon curtailed by rough and ready local punishment as local people took justice into their own hands. Laws were devised for the submission of a claim and methods of settling disputes and codes of behavior and punishment were adopted.

The gold rushes (and silver rushes for that matter) died away as the surface metals were exhausted and more technological and expensive methods were needed to mine out the deeper and more inaccessible deposits. Gold brought people west of the Rockies and although many moved on to new lands, many more stayed behind and settled in the new towns established on prospectors' money.

Above: A row of tents marks the beginnings of Skagway, a boom town in the panhandle of Alaska, which sprang up following the gold rush in the Klondike. Unfortunately for these prospectors, Alaska provided one of the most forbidding climates in which to grapple with the earth.

Right: Gold prospectors panning for alluvial gold below Disc Miller Creek in the Klondike, a region in the western region of the Yukon Territory, c. 1895. Although this last great gold rush was in Canada, most of the miners were American veterans of earlier endeavors.

PART 2

AMERICANS IN POLITICS

THE DEPRESSION

The Great Depression started with the slide of stocks and shares at the Wall Street Stock Exchange on October 24, 1929—"Black Thursday"—and was catapulted into reality by the total collapse of the stock market on October 29. The depression lasted for ten dreadful years before the first signs of recovery, and its effects rippled out from America to cause a worldwide economic slump.

Many causes lay behind the collapse of confidence in the economy: the rich were getting richer at the expense of the poor, manufacture was outstripping consumption—the warehouses were full of unsold goods, there were thousands of small independent banks with inadequate reserves, and America exported huge amounts of goods abroad, funded by U.S. loans because high American tariffs prevented the reciprocation of trade. Finally, the Federal Reserve System encouraged "cheap" money with an easy-lending, low-interest policy, much of which was put into wild stock market speculation. When confidence evaporated and the bubble burst, investors rushed into panic selling, and large speculators liquidated their holdings. Thousands of investors were ruined within hours.

Within three years the economy was completely shattered; industrial production had halved, imports and exports dropped by two-thirds, land prices plummeted, industry and commerce ground to a halt, banks failed, industrialists were ruined, workers laid off, and unemployment soared. Those few who held on to their jobs found their wages ruthlessly cut. Even middle-class professioinals were badly hit and many lost their jobs as well as their homes on which they had unserviceable mortgages.

President Herbert Hoover was deeply concerned, but virtually powerless in the face of such catastrophic collapse. He tried to restore public confidence with reassuring speeches and tried to devise employment by forcing the creation of infrastructure—roads, bridges, and public buildings. He also tried to stabilize crop prices, and even obtained a promise from employers not to reduce wages or

Previous Page: President Woodrow Wilson (1856–1924) with his second wife, Edith Wilson (1872–1961), at the first baseball game of the 1916 season.

Right: Huge crowds outside the Treasury Building watching the Wall Street Stock Exchange across the corner, October 24, 1929. Only one third of the thousands of independent banks were members of the Federal Reserve System—this meant these small banks had no financial backing when customers demanded their money back when the run started.

cut jobs unnecessarily. Misguidedly, he also agreed to raise tariffs to restrict foreign imports. This was self-defeating because the American economy needed foreign money to restimulate business and industry.

However, Hoover steadfastly refused to give national financial unemployment aid through government intervention; this was a matter for state authorities, local employers, and private charity (which had rapidly run out of funds). He believed that federal relief would unbalance the economy and encourage slackness and destroy moral fiber. He believed that the failure was largely in the minds of Americans, not in the economy. He preached this self-reliance message to an increasingly skeptical public for the next three years, by which time he changed his tune to blaming influences outside America for the depression.

Something had to be done, so in January 1932 Hoover proposed a new package of measures. He created the Reconstruction Finance Corporation to lend money to banks and institutions to use to revive the economy, credit facilities were extended, and loans were made to corporations and state

Above: A crowd of men at a labor exchange during the Depression. By July 1932, nearly twenty-five percent of the working population was unemployed.

Right: A man selling pants from a baby carriage on the streets of New York. Photograph dated c. 1930.

Far right: Crowds running through Wall Street following news of the Stock Market crash on October 29, 1929. Before the crash, Americans enjoyed the highest standard of living in the world. On Black Thursday, a record 12.9 million shares changed hands as prices dropped and investors lost fortunes. A similar panic hit the stock exchanges in Los Angeles, Chicago, and San Francisco.

Right: Unemployed men at Al Capone's soup kitchen, November 18, 1930.

Below: A breadline at the intersection of 6th Avenue and 42nd Street in New York City, February 1932. Breadlines were often the only way of getting even meager rations. Although people were starving during the Great Depression, surprisingly few actually starved to death—a reported 110 between 1929 and 1933.

Far Right: Food handouts during the Depression. At this period there were large numbers of itinerants—of both sexes and all ages—wandering around the country from town to town. They lived in makeshift camps and relied on soup kitchens for sustenance.

governments for public works—but absolutely no money for direct federal relief for individuals, although he allowed money to feed farm animals when their owners couldn't afford it.

By now Hoover was hugely unpopular, but the Republican Party had no other candidates and was left with no choice but to nominate him again as its presidential candidate for the 1932 election. He was up against the Governor of New York, Franklin D. Roosevelt, who won by a landslide. In the four-month hand-over period, public faith in the economy wavered badly again. There was another run on money as panic withdrawals bankrupted many banks and thirty-eight states proclaimed an indefinite "bank holiday" as deposits were frozen.

Roosevelt declared a national bank holiday and called Congress into special session. In ten hours, they produced the Emergency Banking Relief Bill, placing all banks under federal control and reopening solvent banks. Then, on March 12, in the first of his radio "fireside chats," Roosevelt told Americans that it was safe to bank their savings. People listened and believed in the "New Deal." Relief was palpable as savings poured back into the reserves and the Depression was on the upturn.

In the period subsequently known as the "Hundred Days," Congress passed a great deal of legislation designed to improve the economy. The highlight

Above: An inhabitant of "Hooverville" in Circleville, Ohio, 1938. Every town had a "Hooverville" on the outskirts, where jobless men lived in cardboard shacks. There they slept wrapped in newspapers known as "Hoover blankets."

Left: A father and his four young children on their verandah, c. 1935. Families lived on charity and handouts, which in the rural South were nonexistent. There was no government unemployment money for the jobless and they had to make good with what little resources they had.

Far left: Farmers in Oklahoma sitting in the shade while their crops burn in the fields during August 1936. Farm prices plummeted and farmers were among the worst off in society. Ironically, although people starved in the cities, crops were plentiful in much of the countryside, but prices had halved, farmers' incomes dropped, and they could not afford to harvest the crops and take them to market. Food was left to rot on the land for lack of money and resources.

Right: Evicted sharecroppers and their possessions along Highway 60, Missouri, January 1939. Cotton was still the main crop in the South and also the most affected by the Depression. Much of it went to export and world prices had dropped. New Deal agricultural policies did little to help African-Americans as Roosevelt depended too much on Southern landholder support to do anything for their civil rights.

was the Federal Emergency Relief Act, authorizing $500 million for direct relief in the form of paid work-relief projects (not in straight unemployment handouts). This was to preserve the dignity of the unemployed by providing paid jobs.

Not only the poor suffered during the depression: the fate of African-Americans was much worse than that of white Americans. They were always the last to be hired and first to be fired. They did benefit in the New Deal along with the white poor. However, by 1935, nearly thirty percent of African-American families were on relief and federal funds were at last targeted to their specific needs, some credit of which should go to Eleanor Roosevelt, who was unusually outspoken against racial discrimination and a fearless champion for civil rights.

POLITICIANS & PRESIDENTS

"I do solemnly swear that I will faithfully execute the Office of President of the United States, and will to the best of my ability, preserve, protect and defend the Constitution of the United States."

The president is the chief executive of the United States of America, and the oath he takes commits him to preserve, protect, and defend the Constitution. Every president has done this, the extent of his success depending on his intelligence and intuitive ability, the strength of his party and political allies, and national and world circumstances beyond his control—above all, it depends on luck.

The president is chosen by the popular vote of the American people. To be eligible for the office, he must be an American by birthright, be at least thirty-five years old, and have lived in the United States for a minimum of fourteen years. The constitution defines and limits his powers, and he does not necessarily enjoy a majority support in the house of Congress, nor is he a member of that body.

At state occasions he is the principal, and it is with the president that ultimate power resides. He is the administrative head of the nation and is responsible for the rule of law. In addition, he is commander-in-chief and the highest ranking officer of the armed forces. However, since 1973 it is Congress that declares war. He is allowed to convene a special session of Congress if he considers it necessary and holds a limited power of veto over Congressional bills but can be overruled by a two-thirds majority in both chambers. Without the majority support of his political party in Congress, the President is unable to enforce his political will, but he can pardon people accused of federal crimes. He can be removed from office by impeachment.

There have been forty-two presidents since the first incumbent, George Washington, in 1789. Of these, three gained office without an election—two after assassinations, Chester A. Arthur and Lyndon B. Johnson (who would be elected a year later in his own right), and one, Gerald Ford, after the resignation of Richard Nixon.

Right: The 25th president, Republican William McKinley (1843–1901), and his wife Ida Saxton McKinley sitting in armchairs, c. 1890. McKinley declared war on Spain after the U.S battleship *Maine* was blown up in Havana harbor while on a courtesy visit. He was assassinated in 1901.

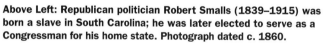

Above Left: Republican politician Robert Smalls (1839–1915) was born a slave in South Carolina; he was later elected to serve as a Congressman for his home state. Photograph dated c. 1860.

Above Right: Franklin Pierce (1804–1869), the 14th president, seen c. 1855. He is considered to have been a weak president although his party, the Democrats, controlled Congress.

Right: President Abraham Lincoln (1809–1865) with General George McClellan (1826–1885) at his headquarters on the battlefield of Antietam, Maryland, October 1862.

Far Right: General Ulysses S. Grant (1822–1885) was one of the most successful Union Army officers. He later served as the 18th president between 1869 and 1877. Although a successful general, he was not a good politician and presided over a corrupt and scandal-ridden administration. A Republican, his term was notable for a law passed by Congress guaranteeing all men the right to vote, regardless of their color. Photograph dated 1864.

PRESIDENTS
OF THE
UNITED STATES OF AMERICA

1.	George Washington	1789-1797
2.	John Adams	1797-1801
3.	Thomas Jefferson	1801-1809
4.	James Madison	1809-1817
5.	James Monroe	1817-1825
6.	John Quincy Adams	1825-1829
7.	Andrew Jackson	1829-1837
8.	Martin van Buren	1837-1841
9.	William Henry Harrison	1841-1841
10.	John Tyler	1841-1845
11.	James K. Polk	1845-1849
12.	Zachary Taylor	1849-1850
13.	Millard Fillmore	1850-1853
14.	Franklin Pierce	1853-1857
15.	James Buchanan	1857-1861
16.	Abraham Lincoln	1861-1865
17.	Andrew Johnson	1865-1869
18.	Ulysses S. Grant	1869-1877
19.	Rutherford B. Hayes	1877-1881
20.	James A. Garfield	1881-1881
21.	Chester A. Arthur	1881-1885
22.	Grover Cleveland	1885-1889
23.	Benjamin Harrison	1889-1893
24.	Grover Cleveland	1893-1897
25.	William McKinley	1897-1901
26.	Theodore Roosevelt	1901-1909
27.	William H. Taft	1909-1913
28.	Woodrow Wilson	1913-1921
29.	Warren G. Harding	1921-1923
30.	Calvin Coolidge	1923-1929
31.	Herbert C. Hoover	1929-1933
32.	Franklin D. Roosevelt	1933-1945
33.	Harry S Truman	1945-1953
34.	Dwight D. Eisenhower	1953-1961
35.	John F. Kennedy	1961-1963
36.	Lyndon B. Johnson	1963-1969
37.	Richard M. Nixon	1969-1974
38.	Gerald Ford	1974-1977
39.	James E. Carter	1977-1981
40.	Ronald Reagan	1981-1989
41.	George H.W. Bush	1989-1993
42.	William J. Clinton	1993-2001
43.	George W. Bush III	2001-

Far Left: Theodore Roosevelt (1858–1919), the 26th president. After two years working as a cowboy in the Wild West, he gained immense popularity for his exploits with the Rough Riders in the Spanish-American War, and thus became the youngest president in American history. Photograph taken in 1905.

Left: Roosevelt with the Scottish-born conservationist John Muir (1838–1914) on Glacier Point in Yosemite, California, 1906.

Below: Calvin Coolidge (1872–1933), later the 30th president, mowing on his father's farm in Plymouth, Vermont, while Governor of Massachusettes and Republican candidate for vice-president, c. 1920.

Left: The 29th president, Warren Gamaliel Harding (1865–1923), center, with the physicist Albert Einstein, left, and Sigmund Freud, c. 1920.

Below: Franklin D. Roosevelt (1882–1945) chats to two Georgia farmers in the year he was elected president, 1932. He is "on the stump"—drumming up support from the voters. A Democrat, he served for a record four terms despite being wheelchair-bound by polio. He won his first term with 57.4 percent of the popular vote, the second with 60.8 percent, his third with 54.8 percent, and his final term with 53.5 percent. His "New Deal" helped pull the United States out of the long years of the Depression by funding the building of public works such as roads, dams, and bridges, and introduced a radical program of social welfare measures bringing much-needed relief to millions of starving people. After the U.S. was forced into World War II, Roosevelt played a crucial role in the Allied international diplomacy and attended the conferences in Casablanca, Cairo, Teheran, and Yalta.

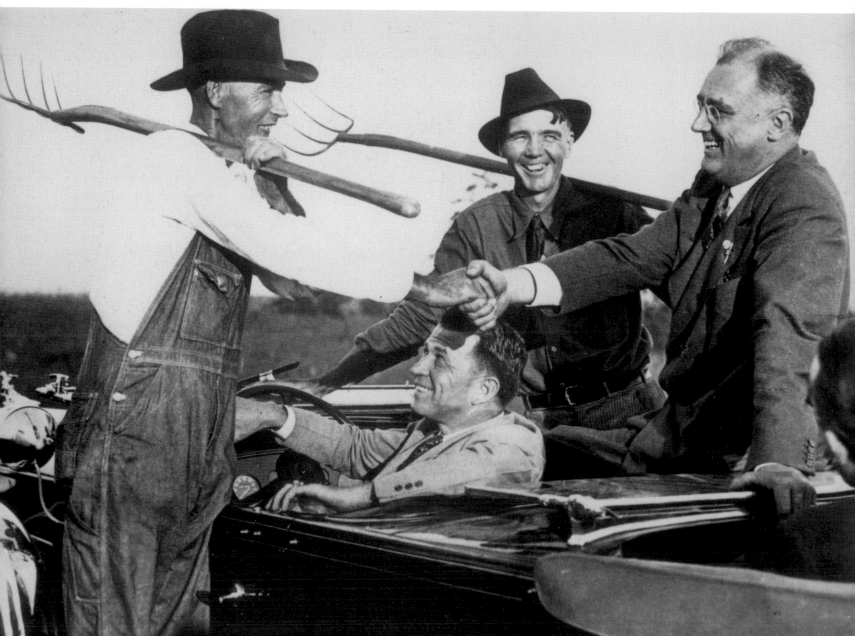

Left: Politician and notorious anti-Communist, Joseph Raymond McCarthy (1908–1957) (second from right) with David Shine, Roy Cohn, and Frank Carr on September 21, 1953. McCarthy led a campaign against supposed Communist subversion in the early 1950s.

Below: American politicians and future presidents (the 37th and 35th, respectively) Richard Milhous Nixon (1913–1994, back row, far right) and John F. Kennedy (1917–1963, back row, second from right) with other freshmen Congressmen in Washington, D.C. in 1947. Kennedy was assassinated in Dallas on November 22, 1963, and Nixon infamously forced to resign in 1974 to avoid the humiliation of impeachment.

Top: The 36th president, Lyndon Baines Johnson, discusses the Voting Rights Act with American clergyman and civil rights campaigner Martin Luther King, Jr. 1965.

Left: JFK campaigning for the presidency in 1959. He eventually won a very close contest against Republican candidate Richard Nixon with 49.7 percent of the popular vote to Nixon's 49.5 percent.

Above: Nixon became the 37th President in 1969 but would quit the White House in ignominy after the Watergate scandal.
Here he is seen briefing politicians before his televised announcement of a cease-fire in the Vietnam War. Left to right: Nixon, Hugh Scott, Tip O'Neill, Carl Albert, Mike Mansfield, Gerald Ford (later 38th President), Spiro Agnew (Nixon's Vice-President), and Henry Kissinger.

LAW & ORDER

The establishment of law and order in a country so vast and diverse as the United States of America was no easy matter. Americans have historically been noted for their individualism, which they interpret as the right to defend themselves and their property against all hostile elements by any means necessary. But this rugged self-dependence could only go so far, and collective responsibility for law and order was quickly established, even in the apparently lawless West, where the rule of law spread almost as rapidly as the settlers. This came about because even the earliest pioneers soon found they needed to organize together to protect themselves from attack by outlaw bands, general civil disturbances, and hostile Native Americans, as well as to be able to get together to help each other in times of natural disasters such as fire, drought, and flood.

Lynching was a common practice on the frontier and in the South. In the West, such mob rule was often the only law around, but in the South it was a defiance of the law when a kangaroo court would trump up charges and summarily lynch a victim. All manner of reasons were given for lynching, with the victim's "crime" often just being in the wrong place at the wrong time. One of the most common reasons for lynching was rape and sexual assault, but this was often used as an excuse for lynching petty criminals. Lynchings peaked in the 1890s after the Civil War with a reported 1,875 incidents, mostly in the South. Between 1889 and 1940, an estimated 3,833 lynchings took place; ninety percent of these took place in the South, and eighty percent of the victims were black.

Local governments across the land were naturally anxious to control the law for themselves and put a halt to incidents such as lynchings. However, they were reluctant to create a European-style police force, which they felt was inappropriate for Americans. However, after the full-scale riots in Philadelphia in 1844 it became obvious that a policing organization was required to control and enforce the peace. Within ten years, all the major cities had started up their own uniformed police force to control the streets.

Right: National Guardsmen called out to quell race riots in Chicago, July 1919. Although race riots were common at this time, the ones in Chicago were particularly bad; thirty-eight people were killed and a further 537 injured. The trouble originally stemmed from the slowdown in immigration and the subsequent shortage of workers in the North. Unemployed African-Americans from the South moved North to fill the shortage, only to meet often-violent protest from poor white workers who feared their job opportunities were being taken away from them.

Unfortunately, these early forces often proved to be factional along religious and ethnic lines. This could become dangerously divisive at times, such as in New York City in 1857 when two rival police forces—one a state force sponsored by Republican nativists and the other a city force supported by Catholic Democrats—actually battled openly against each other in the streets.

The police were there to see that the people adhered to the rights, laws, and freedoms of American citizens as delineated in the Constitution. The American Constitution, as signed by all the member states on September 17, 1787, lays down the framework of rights and freedoms for citizens even against their own government, should that office prove oppressive or unjustifiably restrictive. Furthermore, it guarantees an independent judiciary as a buffer against unreasonable government encroachment, and is the source of ultimate appeal for justice. How these rights and freedoms were interpreted by the law enforcement officers was not always true to the spirit of the work.

One of the earliest covert law enforcement agencies was Pinkerton's Detective Agency, which started during the Civil War by infiltrating undercover agents into Southern camps; by doing this, they earned themselves a sinister reputation. After the war, the agency started working for industrialists, who were anxious to break up organized labor in their mines, steelworks, and factories. The agency supplied infiltrators, spies, strikebreakers, and even gunmen.

The methods of Pinkerton's Agency were used as the blueprint for the Bureau of Investigation when it was set up in 1908 to investigate federal crimes which transgressed state boundaries or endangered national institutions or rule of law. It become the Federal Bureau of Investigation in 1924. As time passed, the FBI's scope was extended to deal with public concerns over the trade in white slaves, kidnapping, and most notoriously, Communist spies when the Bureau was under the control of J. Edgar Hoover in the 1950s.

Another arm of the law is the National Guard. They are part-time, volunteer State military forces, paid for by the government, and partially trained and equipped by them as well. They can be conscripted into the regular armed forces in times of need, and can be ordered into federal service by the President under the authority of the Constitution—as they were in 1940 during World War II when the divisions were mobilized and volunteers became full-time soldiers. The National Guard is used to quell civil unrest and aid the rescue services in time of local and national disaster. It came to international prominence when they were frequently called out during the civil rights protests of the late 1960s and early 1970s.

Left: Scottish-born American detective Allan Pinkerton (seated at right) and several of his security officers, c. 1863. His agents conducted secret service operations for the Union forces during the Civil War. As a cooper in his native Glasgow, Pinkerton became involved in the Chartist movement and his radical views led to a reward being issued for his arrest. Fearing imprisonment, he fled to America where he founded his famous detective agency.

Right: An African-American chain gang in Little Rock, Arkansas, c. 1910. Chain gangs were used to build public amenities and to perform other work such as breaking rocks for roads and digging ditches in areas away from the prison. Prisoners were chained together to make it difficult to escape, while at the same time enabling them to do hard physical work.

Left: Police officer directing traffic while standing on a box in Kearny Street, San Francisco, California, c. 1923.

Below Left: Organized crime—particularly the Mafia—came to the fore during the Prohibition years of the 1920s. The gangsters were hunted both by their enemies in the underworld and the forces of law and order. These American Mafia members are lying low in Sicily.

Right: Sheriff sitting in front of the jail in McAlester, Oklahoma, August 1936.

Below: Striking employees of the Conestoga Transportation Company in Lancaster, Pennsylvannia overturn a car containing six strike-breaking tramcar operators outside the depot, October 10, 1945.

Right: Detective Louis Weiner (left), and Patrolmen Donald Shea and Joseph McClellan (right), who helped to capture Slick Willie Sutton (center). Also known as the "Actor" because he was a master of disguise, Slick Willie was implicated in a number of bank robberies. The police had been hunting him for five years when he was captured early in March 1952.

Far Right: Juan Vasquez, the vice president of the Assassins, a New York street gang, waits outside the gang headquarters on 101st Street in November 1961.

Below: Mrs. Worthington, official dog catcher of Cheltenham Township, chases a French poodle across a lawn with her big net, c. 1955.

Right: The arrest of Lee Harvey Oswald (1939–1963) for the assassination of President Kennedy in Dallas, 1963.

Below: A line of policemen on duty during a black voting rights march in Montgomery, Alabama. Dr. Martin Luther King, Jr. led the march from Selma, Alabama, to the state capitol in Montgomery, March 1965.

Left: Soldiers in Newark, New Jersey, take cover behind police cars while attempting to locate a sniper firing from a window during race riots in the city, 1967.

Below: Secret Service agents surround President Ronald Reagan and members of his entourage after an assassination attempt outside the Hilton Hotel in Washington, D.C., March 30, 1981.

CIVIL RIGHTS

The civil rights movement has a long history in America but its full flowering into a truly widespread, popular movement occured in the 1960s through the early 1970s.

The earliest Civil Rights Bill was passed in March 1866. This gave citizenship to African-Americans and forbade discrimination against citizens on grounds of race or color. To make this unrepealable, the bill's provisions were controversially (in the South) incorporated into the Fourteenth Amendment to the Constitution of April 1866. A further Civil Rights Act in 1875 forbade racial discrimination in public places such as theaters, inns, and on public transportation, but the act was never enforced. African-American civil rights were not respected as the law dictated, and they were rapidly eroded with a number of decisions from the Supreme Court which deprived blacks of the guarantee of the equal rights to which they were already entitled. Social segregation became a reality.

Much of the political discrimination centered around African-American voting rights. Many attempts, both outright illegal and through the courts, were made to thwart black voters from exercising their rights, especially in the South. Congress finally stepped in to ratify the position in August 1957 with another Civil Rights Act which established a Civil Rights Commission to investigate cases of franchise discrimination. It gave power to the Justice Department to sue on behalf of African-American voting rights. Another Civil Rights Act in 1960 extended these provisions, but to little effect in the South where many black citizens were still denied their right to vote.

The civil rights movement really ignited, when, in December 1955 in Montgomery, Alabama, an African-American woman named Rosa Parks refused to give up her seat on a bus to a white man. She was arrested. The local Baptist minister, Martin Luther King Jr., and 50,000 supporters organized a boycott of the local bus companies and despite mass arrests and widespread discrimination, the boycott lasted until November 1956, when the state of Alabama was forced to make segregated buses illegal.

Even at the beginning of the 1960s, a hundred years after the American Civil War freed African-Americans from slavery, many poor black Americans were living in far worse conditions than their white

Right: Vietnam War veterans demonstrating with more than 2,000 peace protestors in The Mall in Washington. Some came to throw their Purple Heart medals into the garden of the White House, April 26, 1971.

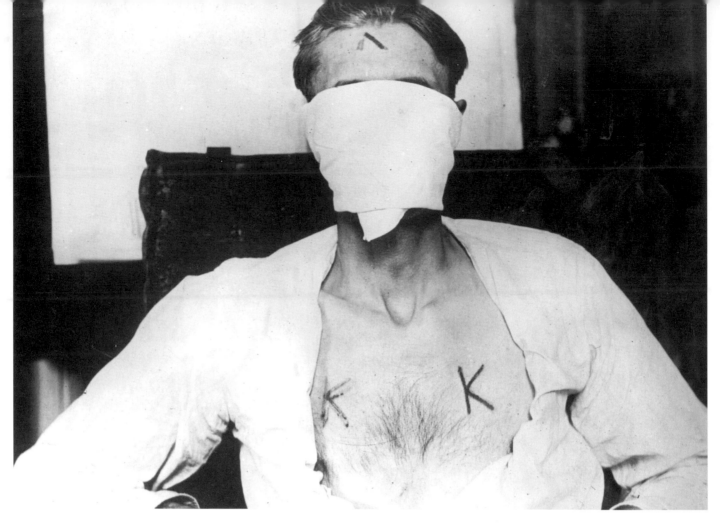

neighbors, and segregation was still commonplace in the South. One of the most important achievements of the early civil rights movement was a widespread campaign to encourage African-Americans to register their vote so as to be able to influence politics locally as well as nationally. In 1963, Martin Luther King, Jr. led thousands of African-Americans in a march on Washington. One of many speakers, he gave his famous "I have a dream" speech. Another speaker on the platform was the singer and dancer Josephine Baker, a tireless campaigner for civil rights.

Many Southern states still denied African-Americans their right to vote and obstructed a new bill in Congress designed to enforce civil rights. Finally, in July 1964 President Johnson, after throwing his considerable weight behind the bill to get it through the Senate, signed the Civil Rights Act of 1964. At a stroke, discrimination against African-Americans anywhere in the United States became illegal—schools were to be desegregated, citizens' voting rights were protected by law, and all federal funds were withheld from any authority that practiced discrimination.

These measures did nothing to alleviate African-American poverty, and the civil rights movement attempted to change this. Nearly one-third of African-Americans lived below the poverty line, a fact exacerbated by the black unemployment rate being twice the national average. Inflation due to the escalating Vietnam War was rising, and the poverty gap widened as blacks found themselves in increasingly deprived schools, houses, and general amenities. Various groups took up the cause, the most prominent of which were the Black Muslims, the Student Nonviolent Coordinating Committee led by Stokely Carmichael, and the Black Panthers.

Above Left: Nelson Burroughs was kidnapped in July 1924 by members of the American white supremacist movement, the Ku Klux Klan, and branded with hot irons because he refused to renounce his Catholic vows. The Ku Klux Klan started as a Southern white supremacist movement to eliminate all foreign—in other words, non-white and non-Protestant—peoples, from America. It was a secretive, sinister movement whose members committed many atrocities, often against African-Americans, but also Catholics, Jews, and foreigners in general. The Klan was founded in Tennessee during 1866 by Confederate veterans, and rapidly spread through the South. After petering out around the turn of the century, it was refounded in 1915 in Georgia by William J. Simmons, a Methodist insurance salesman. The Klan peaked around 1923–24 when it had possibly as many as eight million members. The stronghold of the movement lay in the Northern and Midwestern states, and it dominated affairs in Indiana. Most Klan supporters were blue-collar workers whose homes, jobs, and livelihoods were threatened by immigrants.

Below Left: A gang of white men gather around J. D. Ivy, an African American they blindfolded and tied to a stake in a forest in Georgia on October 3, 1925. Kindling is piled around the victim's feet and doused with kerosene, which will fuel the fire they intend to light. Lynching was a common occurence in the South and often had a racial motive.

Below: African-American passengers getting off the "Freedom Bus" at Dallas, Texas, May 25, 1961.

The civil rights movement of the late 1960s and early 1970s moved on to encompass anti-Vietnam protests. The anti-war marches started in colleges and university campuses in 1965, the issue being particularly relevant to young men of draft age. The war was deeply unpopular among younger, more radical Americans, particularly African-Americans who felt they were sent to Vietnam in disproportionate numbers. Huge protest rallies were held around the country to protest the war and the waste of young lives and money which could otherwise go to alleviate inequality and domestic poverty in the ghettoes. Vietnam was the first war to be brought live and daily by television into the living rooms of America, and the full savagery of war was shown to a horrified audience.

However, the American public as a whole supported the war as a necessary evil against the onsurge of a greater evil—communism. Opinion changed in 1968 after the Tet Offensive intensified the fighting. Increasing unpopularity forced President Johnson to reconsider America's position, and in March he called a partial halt to the bombing of North Vietnam. The peace talks with the North Vietnamese, which eventually led to the American withdrawal from Vietnam, started in Paris in May 1968.

Above: President Lyndon B. Johnson looks over his shoulder and shakes the hand of Dr. Martin Luther King, Jr. at the signing of the Civil Rights Act, Washington D.C., July 2, 1964. The act was a great personal triumph for both men—Martin Luther King, Jr. for raising public awareness and consciousness to such a level that African-American issues were at the forefront of the national agenda, and President Johnson for wholeheartedly bludgeoning Congress into passing the act which had been stuck in the Senate for three months due to a determined Southern filibuster. The act was the most far-reaching of its kind ever passed; it protected African-American voting rights, hastened desegregation, entirely prohibited racial discrimination and stopped federal money going to any organization or group practicing discrimination.

Right: Martin Luther King, Jr. and his wife Loretta Scott King leading a civil rights march from Selma, Alabama, to the state capitol in Montgomery, Alabama, in March 1965. King's philosophy of civil disobedience through passive resistance proved enormously effective and encouraged many to join his protests who had previously been put off by violent radical action. Three years later, Martin Luther King, Jr. was assassinated at his motel in Tennessee on April 4, 1968, while campaigning to improve working conditions for African-Americans in local government.

Above: A military policeman with fixed bayonet keeps pace with protesters in the Alabama civil rights march led by Dr. Martin Luther King, Jr., March 24, 1965.

Left: A woman wearing the robes and hood of the Ku Klux Klan holding her baby at a Klan meeting in Beaufort, South Carolina, May 24, 1965. The Klan reemerged in the early days of the civil rights movement. Only native-born Christian Americans were eligible to join the society with its elaborate secret rituals and regalia. The Klan attracted militant white patriots and although primarily a Southern movement, had adherents across the country, especially in the Midwest, the Southwest, along the Pacific coast and in cities like Dallas, Detroit, and Minneapolis.

Above Right: Black Panthers march to a news conference in New York to protest at the trial of one of their members, Huey P. Newton. Newton was later convicted for the manslaughter of an Oakland policeman, July 22, 1968. The Black Panthers were a radical paramilitary organization founded in Oakland, California, in 1966. Their slogan "Black Power" was the rallying call to many young militant blacks and was heard during violent confrontations with the police. Their chief spokesperson was Eldridge Cleaver.

Right: A group of hippies taunt policeman at the Democratic National Convention of 1968, during the trial of the Chicago Seven, a group of radicals arrested during the protests against the Vietnam War.

Left: Vietnam War veterans pile their military decorations at the base of the statue of the first Chief Justice of the U.S. Supreme Court, John Marshall (1755–1835), in front of the White House on Capitol Hill, Washington, April 26, 1971. The vets were bitterly disillusioned and felt let down by the government in their treatment when they returned bruised and damaged by their horrific experiences in Indochina.

Above: Members of a Gay Rights march on Fifth Avenue, New York. Reverend John Kuiper (right) was the first gay man in America to win the right to adopt a child. He is with his partner, Roger Hooverman, on July 7, 1979. In the 1970s, gay rights became one of the biggest civil rights issues in America, and protestors again took their views to the streets and the ballot box where the "pink vote" was sufficiently important to influence politics. The movement was not always peaceful; there was a riot at Stonewall Bar in New York City in 1969 when gay activists fought back against long-standing police harassment.

PROHIBITION

The sale of alcoholic beverages became illegal in the United States in 1920, when a prohibition amendment to the Constitution was passed. The law was the culmination of a long campaign led by the Temperance movement, whose members regarded alcohol as an instrument of the devil and a barrier to salvation. Other reformers wanted alcohol banned because of the social evils it was believed to produce—crime, lawlessness, prostitution, gambling, and ultimately, poverty.

Americans were traditionally heavy drinkers—they were well known for it and foreign visitors frequently commented on the amount they drank. In reaction, the American Society for the Promotion of Temperance was founded in Boston in 1826 and the movement started gathering momentum. The Prohibition campaign encapsulated many different aims—those of wives and mothers to stop drunkenness and abuse, employers to stop drunkenness at work, the church to prevent moral lassitude, protect child welfare, and prevent vice of all kinds, and social reformers, who regarded the liquor industry as too rich and powerful and riddled with corruption. By 1915, nineteen states had a prohibition on the sale and consumption of liquor, in addition to which many towns and counties had local prohibition restrictions.

When America joined the war in Europe, the prohibition movement gained fresh impetus, with campaigners claiming patriotic necessity to enforce anti-drink laws. Alcohol reduced workers' and soldiers' ability to think and work efficiently, and furthermore, the grain saved from alcohol production could instead go into the food supply. Success was achieved in December 1917 when Congress passed the 18th Amendment (known as the Volstead Act of 1919 after the Congressman who introduced it) prohibiting "the manufacture, sale, or transportation of intoxicating liquors." This was ratified the following month and became effective on January 16, 1920. Immediately, thousands of illegal stills were smashed and confiscated and millions of gallons of wines and spirits poured away.

Right: Men destroying wine and spirits in Boston in 1920 during Prohibition. Organized crime quickly established its own breweries and distilleries to capitalize on the fiscal opportunities for making and moving money around without government or federal interference. It has been calculated that $2 billion of legal distilling, brewing, and retail business went out of public circulation into professional organized crime.

The prison population soared as bootleggers were incarcerated and federal governments lost huge amounts of tax revenue.

On top of this, Prohibition proved impossible to enforce. There were too few (and badly paid) enforcement officers to cope with the huge popular demand for alcohol. In small towns and rural areas, the law was followed, but in the big cities, especially German and Irish immigrant areas, the alcohol laws were unpopular and widely ignored. The worst side effect was the rise in organized crime. This started with bootleggers making a fortune running illegal alcohol operations across all the borders of the United States, but branched out into racketeering, gambling, and prostitution. Ultimately, Prohibition gave organized crime the financial muscle to establish its presence in all levels of society, an evil which took many years to eradicate.

From the start, there were demands for repeal of the 18th Amendment, and even though many supporters admitted it was a partial failure, they strongly resisted repeal. The turning point was the Great Depression. Repeal, it was argued, would revive the economy by allowing a liquor tax, provide a million jobs in the brewing and distilling industries, and give the ailing farmers a market for their grain crops.

When the Democrats won the 1932 election, in part on a repeal ticket, Roosevelt became President and Congress immediately passed the 21st Amendment, which repealed the 18th. The 21st Amendment became law on December 5, 1933, just in time for Christmas. The decision to prohibit alcohol reverted to individual States, only seven of which voted to retain the ban.

Above: Contraband beer being spilled into the streets from barrels in 1925. Beer was also brewed illegally for private consumption.

Above Left: 33,100 gallons of wine being flushed into the gutter outside the North Cucamonga Winery in Los Angeles at the start of Prohibition in February 1920. World War I finally gave prohibitionists the leverage they needed to get their ideas through Congress. Anti-German feeling was rife and many brewers were believed to be German. Furthermore, beer and whiskey used up valuable grain stocks which could be sent to feed the soldiers. The Prohibitionists' first triumph was to force Congress to pass a law forbidding the manufacture and consumption of alcohol for the duration of the war.

Left: Barrels lined up by the side of a road in an American town where alcohol was found and confiscated during 1925. Hugely alcoholic "moonshine" and "mountain dew" were made illegally in stills across the country. Demand for alcohol was so great that even industrial alcohol was redistilled into ersatz gin and whiskey, sometimes with tragic results.

Top: Evening-dressed revelers buying their drinks at a bar during Prohibition in November 1931. By 1929, 32,000 speakeasies were scattered across New York—double the number of saloons before Prohibition started. By 1933, they had dropped to 9,000, but that was due mainly to the Depression. Many speakeasies had gambling tables and had to pay protection money to organized crime to keep the law—and other racketeers—away. However, speakeasies held the lure of dangerous glamor for many of their richer clients. There they could rub shoulders with ruthless criminals and dazzling call girls, and feel excitingly risqué and sophisticated—while paying huge amounts for their drinks.

Above: A government official swings an axe on untaxed alcohol ready for shipment in 1950. Well after the repeal of the Prohibition laws, alcohol was still a prime interest for criminals as it could generate large amounts of untaxed money for racketeers.

Right: American men guarding their private beer brewing hideout during 1935. Rural America, especially the Bible Belt, provided the backbone of the Prohibition movement.

PART 3   AMERICANS AT WAR

CIVIL WAR

The American Civil War was not caused simply by slavery—although it became the signature issue. This bloody civil war was based on the great divide between the agrarian South and industrial North that had widened since the start of the Industrial Revolution. Regional differences were personified by the Federal tariffs imposed on imported goods that could be manufactured in the North. The North looked to the South as a market for its manufactured goods, but it was often cheaper for the South to purchase the goods abroad—but not after the tariffs were imposed. In 1832, when South Carolina refused to collect tariffs, Federal troops were sent in.

The issue of slavery, which would became—particularly with hindsight—in the popular view the main cause of the Civil War, was only one of many issues on which the North and South differed. Indeed, Lincoln had been elected in 1860 without promising to free the slaves. When the war began, his goal was preservation of the Union, not abolition of slavery. Even after the war began, he used his promise not to interfere with slavery as an inducement to persuade the Confederacy to rejoin the Union. For its part, the Confederate States of America banned the importation of slaves in 1861, and had enacted a measure emancipating its slaves before the war ended.

Simply, by 1861, North and South had evolved as different and separate nations. The South, which did not have the capability or desire to dominate the North, declared itself separate. Thus began the conflict which the North called "the Civil War," while the South fought what it called "the War for Southern Independence."

The first shot was fired in anger at Fort Sumter on April 12, 1861. The end—in effect, if not in reality—took place on April 9, 1865, when the South's greatest general, Robert E. Lee, surrendered at Appomattox. It was—in terms of percentage of population killed—the bloodiest conflict in American history. While World War II deaths exceeded those of the Civil War, they did so only barely. In percentage terms, World War II was responsible for the death of one percent of the population, the Civil War three percent.

It was bloody, bitter, and—as with every civil war—the wounds took a long time to heal.

Previous Page: Union General William Tecumseh Sherman and members of his staff before the siege of Atlanta, Georgia, 1864.

Right: A splendid view of part of the Union Army at the start of the war in 1861. This is the 96th Pennsylvania Infantry Regiment lined up for inspection at a camp near Washington.

Above: Confederate volunteers at Warrington Navy Yard, Pensacola, Florida. Florida was one of the slave-holding states that seceded —on February 1, 1861. On May 9, 1862, the Union commander responsible for Florida, Georgia, and South Carolina took it upon himself to abolish slavery there without Lincoln's knowledge. This drove many to ally themselves to the Confederates, but in the end Florida played little part in the war and surrendered in early May 1865.

Right: A powder monkey on board the Union warship *New Hampshire* off the South Carolina coast. "Powder monkeys" were young boys who brought powder charges to the gun crews. The Federal navy was always more powerful than that of the South and was able to blockade the Southern states effectively.

Far Right: Artillery and cannon balls in Virginia in preparation for the campaign of 1862. Artillery was the greatest killer of troops in action during the Civil War and responsible for battering many forts into submission.

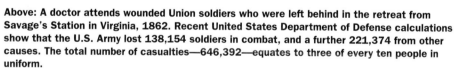

Above: A doctor attends wounded Union soldiers who were left behind in the retreat from Savage's Station in Virginia, 1862. Recent United States Department of Defense calculations show that the U.S. Army lost 138,154 soldiers in combat, and a further 221,374 from other causes. The total number of casualties—646,392—equates to three of every ten people in uniform.

Right: The camp of the Chief Ambulance Officer of the Ninth Army Corps near Petersburg, Virginia, 1864. Petersburg was the key supply center for Richmond, the capital of the Confederacy. If it fell, Lee would be forced to withdraw. Between June 15 and 18, 1864, Grant threw the entire weight of his Union forces against Petersburg and then began a siege operation. The city would hold out until April 1865.

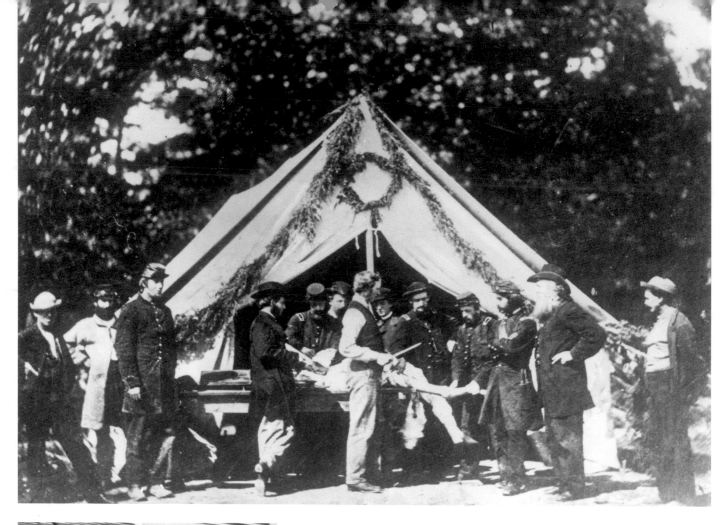

Left: A surgical tent at Gettysburg, Pennsylvania. It has been said that no more important battle was fought between Waterloo and the Marne than the one at Gettysburg. It was certainly the turning point in the Civil War. At 3 p.m. on July 2, 1863, 13,000 Confederate infantry led by Major General George E. Pickett marched in formation across the open ground toward Cemetery Ridge. They met a wall of fire. Thousands fell, and although a handful reached the Union lines, they were forced to fall back. Lee admitted defeat and the next day withdrew his army. It was the bloodiest battle of the war, and claimed 28,000 Confederate and 23,000 Union casualties.

Below Left: African-American troops in the Union Army, 1865. Black troops had to fight Union prejudice as well as rebel bullets, but when they did see action they fought with valor and distinction, notably at such battles as Milliken's Bend, Port Hudson, Fort Wagner, and Nashville.

Right: Crippled Union soldiers and their nurses at the Armory Square Hospital at Washington, D.C., 1865.

Below: Soldiers in a burial party at Cold Harbor rest on a gun carriage, 1864.

A Ward in Armory Square Hospital Washington, D.C.

INDIAN WARS

The story of the Indian Wars is one of the least palatable in American history. It is estimated that the native population fell from five million to some 250,000 in the 400 years after Columbus reached the New World. Over the same period, the white population grew from none to seventy-five million. Unsurprisingly, much of the reduction of Native American numbers was not due to warfare; starvation, disease, and poverty played their part as each tribe was coerced onto reservations, many of which could not sustain the numbers sent there. But there were also battles, as many of the proud tribes fought U.S. forces—particularly after the Civil War ended. Sioux, Apache, Ute, Cheyenne, Nez Perce—they and many more tribes ensured the Western frontier areas of the United States needed a military presence.

The size of the areas involved and the speed of their enemies' movements meant that U.S. forces tended to be cavalry units garrisoned at key forts. At first—before the Civil War—there were few mounted units available, and those were withdrawn to the East and formed into six cavalry regiments. Until their return, the plains were patrolled by volunteers.

In 1865, the cavalry returned to an area boiling over with troubles. On July 28, 1866, four new cavalry regiments—the 7th through 10th—were raised, the 9th and 10th being unusual for the time, being composed of black troops led by white officers. These forces were able to suppress the tribes that resisted the government's policy of herding the Native Americans onto isolated reservations. While it would be untrue to say that the U.S. forces had it all their own way—think of the Battle of the Little Big Horn—the West was pacified by 1890, after the surrender of Geronimo's Apaches and the death of the last Sioux warriors at the Battle of Wounded Knee.

Right: Civil War veteran General W. T. Sherman and the Peace Commission meet at Fort Laramie in Wyoming, May 1868, to try and end the Red Cloud War between the Lakota Sioux and U.S. forces. The resulting treaty secured the removal of U.S. troops from several Powder River forts, as well as the promise of preserving Powder River Valley as a Sioux hunting ground. Eight years later, war flared again as Sioux land was encroached upon. General Crook led his forces against the Sioux and their Cheyenne allies and on June 25, 1876, part of this force, led by General George Custer, would be annihilated at the Little Big Horn River.

Above: Cavalry units at Fort Custer in the heart of Sioux country, just a few miles from the site of the Battle of the Little Big Horn. The photo was taken in 1877, a year after the battle. It was during this year that Crazy Horse surrendered; Sitting Bull would do so in 1881.

Above Right: Native American prisoners at Fort Marion, Florida. Established in 1870, Fort Marion's dungeons were used to house many Native Americans who had fought against the U.S. Army. This 1875 photograph shows some of the twenty-six Kiowas who had been punished for their resistance by exile from Fort Sill to the dungeons. Later, in 1886, Geronimo and his surviving warriors would also be sent there after surrendering.

Right: Four significant Sioux chiefs with their interpreter in 1885. At the back: Juilis Meyer (interpreter) and Red Cloud, who fought successfully against the whites in the late 1860s. In front: Sitting Bull (see below), and two of the Brulé band, Swift Bear and Spotted Tail, who was murdered on the Rosebud reservation in 1881.

Left: Sitting Bull, or Tatanka Iyotake (c. 1834–90), was the leader of the Hunkpapa band of Western (Lakota) Sioux, and one of the best-known leaders of the resistance against white incursions onto Native American lands. Sitting Bull led the Sioux in the Sioux War of 1876–77, defeated General Custer at Little Big Horn, and escaped to Canada. He surrendered on July 20, 1881, was held prisoner for two years, and was killed in 1890 during the Ghost Dance uprising.

Above: A Gros Ventre war party surveying a small encampment in Montana, 1908. The Atsina—an Algonkian tribe of the northern Plains—became known as the "Gros Ventre" (large belly) tribe, it seems, because their name in sign language involved moving their hands over their abdomen as if showing hunger. Allies of the Blackfoot, today they share the Fort Belknap reservation in Montana with the Assiniboine.

Right: General George Crook (third from right, 1829–90) holds council with the Apache leader Geronimo (center left, 1829–1909). The talks led to the end of the Apache War in March 1886. The Chiricahua Apache had lived on the west side of the Rio Grande in New Mexico, Arizona, and Mexico. By 1853 most of this land had been transferred from Mexico to the United States, and the Government tried to put the Apache on reservations. Hostilities continued until 1886 when Geronimo and his men surrendered. They were imprisoned, but later released and Geronimo became a farmer in Oklahoma.

Left: The original caption reads, "A group of prisoners from the Crow tribe who are being confined to a reservation while colonists take over large tracts of their land. The Crow formerly allied themselves with the settlers against the Sioux, but were ultimately treated in the same way as the resisting tribes." Over 8,000 went to the Crow Reservation established by the 1868 Laramie Treaty. Devastated by smallpox, by 1944 their numbers had fallen to 2,467. Today, however, the Crow have grown in numbers, and over 6,600 live on the Montana reservation.

SPANISH - AMERICAN WAR

The Spanish-American War of 1898 marked a major change in the position of the United States in the world. Until then, apart from the sandbagging of Mexico fifty years earlier, Americans had enough to think about at home—a bloody civil war, massive industrialization, clearing the plains of the indigenous Native American population, and dealing with the massive expansion of immigration. In the 1890s, the American view of the outside world changed. First, the Sino-Japanese War of 1895 had caused concern. The United States had opened Japan up to the commercial world between 1852 and 1854 and felt proprietorial about the country. Then there was acquisition by several European powers of Chinese ports. The United States felt that it should have a part in the action—and would help crush the Boxer Rebellion that started in 1899, then pushed to ensure that China stayed open to trade by all commercial partners rather than Old World colonial powers.

As well as an increasing involvement in world politics, there were other factors working toward U.S. involvement in a war in the Caribbean. The Royal Navy, worried about threats from Germany, had recalled its Caribbean Squadron. Cuba—so often important in U.S. history—had been in revolt against its Spanish masters for many years, and the popular press, particularly that part controlled by William Randolph Hearst, had whipped Americans up against the excesses of Spanish colonialism. On top of all this, there was a presidential election due when the battleship U.S.S. *Maine* entered Havana harbor on a courtesy visit. On February 15, 1898, *Maine* blew up. The reason for the explosion is still a mystery—but it wasn't to Hearst, the American people, and President McKinley, who declared war on Spain.

It was a short war. By July 17, 1899, the Spanish forces in Santiago had surrendered. In the peace treaty that followed, Cuba received its independence from Spain, and the United States its first colonies—Guam, Puerto Rico, and the Philippines, although the Filipinos would fight against U.S. colonial power for well into the twentieth century before being subjugated. Winners in the affair were McKinley, who was reelected in 1900, and Theodore Roosevelt, his Vice-President. Assistant Secretary of the Navy when the war started, Roosevelt had raised a volunteer cavalry regiment—the "Rough Riders"—and became a national hero for his exploits. He would become President in 1901 following McKinley's assassination.

Right: Theodore Roosevelt (center) with his men of the 1st Cavalry Volunteers—the "Rough Riders"—on San Juan Hill during the Spanish-American War, July 1898.

Above: Troops from the 71st Regiment wearing uniforms and carrying rifles, walking up the steps of the Armory upon their return from fighting in Cuba during the Spanish-American War, southeast corner of 34th Street and Park Avenue, New York City.

Left: William McKinley (1843-1901) the 25th President. He led the country to victory in the Spanish-American War, but was assassinated in Buffalo in 1901. His successor, Theodore Roosevelt, took control of a nation coming of age, at the start of what many people have described as the "American Century." Roosevelt would receive the Nobel Peace Prize in 1906 for his brokering of the treaty ending the Russo-Japanese War, would build up United States military power, particularly the U.S. Navy, and started the building of the Panama Canal.

Right: Spanish sailors loading a gun aboard a Spanish cruiser during the Spanish-American War.

Above: U.S. soldiers in a trench near Manila, capital of the Philippines, during the Spanish-American war.

Left: Members of Squadron A riding on horseback during the parade for U.S. naval hero Admiral George Dewey. They were in front of the Croton Distributing Reservoir at Fifth Avenue and 42nd Street, New York City, when the photograph was taken. Dewey oversaw the destruction of the Spanish fleet in Manila Bay, thereby ending the Spanish-American War without loss. A career naval officer, Dewey had graduated from the U.S. Naval Academy in Annapolis and served with Admiral David Farragut during the Civil War thirty-five years earlier.

Right: The men of the 10th Pennsylvania Regiment parading down Fifth Avenue, New York, in 1899 after the successful conclusion of the Spanish-American War.

WORLD WAR I

The U.S. Army changed dramatically between the Civil War and World War I. The Federal Army of 1865 had been large—over a million men—but its weaponry had not changed to any great degree from that of the War of Independence. The infantryman's main weapon was the rifled musket and the main artillery piece was the "Napoleon"—a smoothbore twelve-pounder. By 1918, the U.S. Army's Expeditionary Force in Europe, commanded by General "Black Jack" Pershing, was a highly competent force equipped with modern weapons—tanks, aircraft, machine guns, and artillery. When the Armistice of November 11, 1918 ended the "Great War," the American forces had punched substantially into German lines, and were close to entering Germany itself. For the first time, the New World had come to the rescue of the Old.

The United States Army had learned a lot from the Spanish-American War of 1898, the fighting in the Philippines and China in the early years of the 20th century, and from the attempt to capture Pancho Villa in Mexico. New weapons—the M1911 Colt .45 automatic, the Browning Automatic Rifle, the M1903 six-shot .30 rifle, and machine guns—equipped a force whose officers had been trained in proper officers' schools at Fort Leavenworth, Kansas, or Fort McNair, Washington D.C. The blue uniforms of the Civil War had been replaced by khaki and the combat soldier's personal equipment had been standardized.

America did not want to go to war—Woodrow Wilson had been reelected in 1916 on a no-war ticket. It was the German submarine campaigns that forced the issue, exemplified graphically by the torpedoing in May 1915 of the passenger liner *Lusitania*, with the loss of nearly 1,200 lives, including 124 Americans, and the *Sussex*, a cross-Channel ferry in March 1916. The President's ultimatum that Germany would be held "strictly accountable" for further losses

maintained the status quo until January 1917 when another submarine offensive brought the United States into the war. The Senate and the House approved entry into the war in early April, and Wilson received approval to institute conscription.

Under the command of Pershing, the Expeditionary Force—and its million "Doughboys"—trained extensively in 1917 and early 1918, seeing action at the Aisne and Marne during Germany's last-ditch Spring Offensive. Pershing then attacked, launching the St. Mihiel and then the Meuse-Argonne offensives, the later of which had reached the Belgian border when the war ended.

Right: American soldiers in a gas attack drill in France, 1917. The Chemical Warfare Service was authorized on June 28, 1918.

Far Left: Soldiers crowd the decks of a U.S. troopship during World War I. In the end, over one million "Doughboys" would be sent to Europe, but many arrived too late to see action. The American Expeditionary force suffered 264,000 casualties, including 50,000 killed in battle and almost as many killed by disease.

Left: A blindfolded man picks out draftees by means of a lottery. Under the Selective Service Act of May 18, 1917, every man between twenty-one and thirty had to register for national service. Each man received a number which was entered in the lottery.

Below: American tanks advancing in northern France, 1918. The U.S. Army used French and British vehicles during the war. This is a Renault Light Tank, the type that served in the tank brigade commanded by George Patton—later General and commander of the U.S. Third Army in World War II.

WORLD WAR II

The colossal scale of involvement of U.S. forces in World War II is even more surprising when placed against its unpreparedness when the war in Europe started. In 1939, the U.S. Army had 176,000 men; in 1940, it had 269,000. By 1945 it had grown to eight million. In 1940 the U.S. Navy had just over 200,000 men; in 1945 the number was over four million. At peak strength the U.S. Air Force had 75,000 aircraft and nearly 2,500,000 personnel; the U.S. Marines had 450,000 men. The sheer weight of these figures and the massive organization needed to train them, get them into the field, and arm and sustain them while they were there, speaks volumes for the sacrifices made by the country in those years. The sacrifice in terms of casualties is sobering: 234,874 soldiers, 52,173 airmen, and 36,900 sailors gave their lives during the conflict.

A great power before the war, at the end of the war the United States had become the most powerful country in the world. Its economy had funded the defeat of fascism; its industrial base had produced the weapons; its armies had cleared the Axis forces from the Pacific and had helped liberate Europe.

It was the unprovoked attack by Japanese warplanes on Pearl Harbor on December 7, 1941, that led to U.S. entry into a war that had been raging since September 1939. Japanese strategist Admiral Isoroku Yamamoto—himself opposed to alliance with Germany and a war against the United States—risked all in one daring attack on the U.S. fleet in harbor. A brilliant strategy, but it failed in its immediate objective. The U.S. carriers were preserved and naval air power would defeat the Japanese fleet in the great sea battles of the Coral Sea, Midway, and Leyte Gulf. U.S. sea power allowed a brilliant, if costly, campaign of amphibious landings on the Pacific islands that was halted when Japan surrendered after two atomic bombs heralded a new age of warfare.

In Europe, U.S. involvement started with Air Force attacks on the Third Reich. By the end, B-17 Flying Fortresses escorted by P-51 Mustangs and P-47 Thunderbolts would deprive Germany of its industry. Amphibious landings on the North African coast (Operation "Torch"), Sicily ("Husky"), Italy ("Avalanche"), and finally, Normandy ("Overlord") led to the campaigns that rolled up the German armies. World War II was over; the Cold War beginning.

Right: American troops carry equipment ashore from landing craft at Omaha Beach on June 9, 1944, three days after D-Day heralded the Allied landings along the coast of Normandy.

Above: American howitzers shell German forces retreating near Carentan, France, July 11, 1944. On July 25, after a massive bombardment by artillery and air forces, General Bradley's First Army broke out of the Normandy Beachhead through Operation "Cobra." Patton's Third Army exploited the hole in the German defenses and France was liberated after four years of Nazi rule.

Right: Navy mechanics work on an engine at the Naval Air Training Center, Corpus Christi, Texas, 1942. Naval air power won the war at sea in the Pacific, enabling the U.S. Marines and Army units to conduct their campaign of amphibious landings, leapfrogging from island chain to island chain.

Far Right: Left to right, the officer's winter uniform, the officer's summer uniform and the uniform of an auxiliary—three official uniforms of the U.S. Women's Army Auxiliary Corps being modeled in Washington D.C. on June 4, 1942. Over 300,000 women were employed in the U.S. armed forces, including Women's Airforce Ferry Pilots, who ferried aircraft from factories to units, the U.S. Marine Corps, and the Women's Reserve.

Top: American troops jump from a landing craft and wade through water onto a beach under a dark cloud-streaked sky in Sicily, 1943. After success in the desert war and the evacuation of German troops to Europe in May 1943, the next steps in the war against the Third Reich were the invasions of Sicily on July 10 and Italy on September 3, 1943. The "soft underbelly" of Europe proved to be no such thing. U.S. General Mark Clark (1896–1984) and his Fifth Army would have to fight on until early May 1945.

Above: GIs standing along the barrel of a captured German railway gun, April 1945. Probably the best-known of the German rail guns were "Anzio Annie" and the "Anzio Express." Both were 280mm guns which fired 564 lb. shells during the battles around Anzio in late January 1944.

Right: U.S. Marine raiders in Bougainville, Solomon Islands, February 1944. The Solomons were taken by the Japanese in early 1942. U.S. forces landed there in November 1943, and quickly bypassed the Japanese forces to take the islands and build an airstrip from which they could attack Rabaul. The surrounded Japanese on Bougainville would fight on into 1945.

KOREA

Korea was the forgotten war until a 1974 film and the subsequent television series reminded a new generation of the sacrifices made by an international United Nations force in the early 1950s. The seeds of the Korean War were sown in 1945 when the Japanese forces occupying the country surrendered to the U.S. Army south of the 38th Parallel and to the Red Army to the north. This led to the creation of two Korean states, and a border where the Cold War got hot on June 25, 1950. On that date the North Korean People's Army invaded the south. Reinforced by U.S. troops from Japan, the South Korean Army was nevertheless pushed back into the Pusan perimeter—a small area on the extreme southeast of the peninsula. The U.N. forces came from fifty-three countries, although the bulk were American. On September 15 and 16, 1950, General Douglas MacArthur's (1880–1964) brilliantly-conceived counterattack plan saw the Eighth Army breaking out of the Pusan Perimeter while U.N. amphibious forces landed at Inchon, west of Seoul.

The North Korean Army was pushed north, toward the Yalu River border with China. The Chinese made it clear that any attempt to follow the North Korean Army would bring them into the war. That happened on November 25, when nearly 200,000 Chinese troops attacked, overrunning the U.N. troops and retaking South Korea's capital of Seoul. To make matters worse, in April 1951 General MacArthur was relieved of his command by President Truman after he had demanded the power to bomb China—it is said with nuclear weapons—use Formosan troops against the communists, and blockade the Chinese coast.

His place was taken by General Matthew Ridgway (1895-1993), who had commanded the 18th Airborne Corps in World War II. Under Ridgway the position stabilized, the Chinese were pushed back to the 38th Parallel, and after two further massive Chinese attacks had been withstood, a war of attrition started with lines of trenches, artillery duels, and interminable peace negotiations.

In the end, the peace talks at Kaesong prevailed and the war ended on July 27, 1953. It had seen the deaths of 72,500 U.N. troops, with an additional 84,000 captured or missing. Many of those captured did not see freedom again, dying in captivity.

Right: An American soldier patrolling the streets of Inchon after its capture. Photograph is dated October 7, 1950, some three weeks after the landings.

Above: Actress Marilyn Monroe (1926–1962) entertaining troops in Korea, 1952. Still in the early days of her career, Monroe would make two of her best films the next year, *How to Marry a Millionaire* and *Gentlemen Prefer Blondes*.

Right: A U.S. Army artillery unit in action in the region of Taejon, South Korea, during the September 1950 offensive.

Opposite Page, Above: A GI relaxing on a heap of kit-bags, shortly after the invasion and capture of Inchon, October 7, 1950.

Below and Opposite Page, Below: The beaches of Inchon on September 16, 1950, the day after the first landings. After their experiences in the Pacific and Europe, the U.S. military were the experts on amphibious warfare. The landings at Inchon by 1st Marine Division, USMC, proved this dramatically. Within ten days of the landings they had achieved a linkup with the U.S. Eighth Army and the drive to the Yalu was on.

VIETNAM

The Vietnam War was one of the most traumatic episodes in American history. Until Vietnam, with the possible exception of the Philippines campaign, the United States had refrained from involvement in military action unless the cause was dire—world peace in 1916, to conquer fascism in 1941, and as a result of a U.N. mandate for the Korean War. The Vietnam War was unlike these wars, and caused intense problems within the United States itself—both from civilians who thought the war wasn't worth fighting and the returning draftees who found themselves vilified, their sacrifice overlooked, and—it seemed to many—their captive comrades left to the same fate suffered by so many of the Korean War captives.

It is possible that only now, some thirty years later, a real analysis of the war and its effects can be achieved in a country that has honored its dead with the Vietnam Wall in Washington, D.C. and has accepted a draft dodger as President.

American involvement in Vietnam was the result of the German conquest of France in 1940. Absence of French power allowed the Japanese to move into Indochina where they were resisted by the communist Viet Minh, who were effectively in control of the country in 1945 when the Japanese surrendered and the French returned in force to their erstwhile colony. The United States, afraid that a communist Indochina would see the whole area turn against the West, supported France and, when the French pulled out after their disastrous defeat at Dien Bien Phu, American "advisors" went to South Vietnam—by the end of 1963 there were 16,300 U.S. "advisors" and support troops in Vietnam.

The incident that led to full U.S. involvement took place in the Gulf of Tonkin on August 2, 1964, when first the U.S.S. *Maddox* and then other U.S. Navy vessels were said to have been attacked by North Vietnamese torpedo boats. President Johnson ordered retaliatory air strikes and the U.S. Congress gave him a mandate to wage war. It would take four years of war, fought against a rising crescendo of protest at home, before peace talks began in 1968. In 1969, President Nixon began troop withdrawals, and on August 11, 1972, the last U.S. ground troops left. It was the first time the United States had ever lost a war. Nearly 56,000 Americans had lost their lives. Then, to make matters worse, South Vietnam surrendered to the North in April 1975.

Right: American soldiers during the war, June 27, 1966.

The Vietnam War saw the helicopter come of age as a weapon of war. It was used everywhere—to move troops, to insert special forces, for casualty evacuation, as a spotter for artillery, for heavy lift, for anti-submarine warfare, for air-sea rescue, as gunships, for liaison, and in "psyops" (psychological warfare operations). In short, the helicopter was ubiquitous in Vietnam. Indeed, nearly 5,000 of them were lost, almost half due to enemy action.

Right: U.S. Air Force Sergeant Paul J. Volges in a helicopter winch being assisted by Staff Sergeant William Johnson, October 30, 1967.

Left: Pfc. Carl Aster of the 2nd Battalion, 7th Marine Regiment, on duty in Vietnam in 1968. Behind him a Boeing Vertol CH-46 Sea Knight awaits its next operation.

Below: American troops from the 73rd Airborne Brigade carrying a wounded soldier onto a helicopter near Vung Tau, August 22, 1966. The helicopter is a Bell UH-1 Huey.

Far Left: American soldiers playing baseball in the Vietnamese village of Nui Kinson, March 27, 1968.

Left: A Marine with his pet puppy in Vietnam, c. 1968.

Below: By June 27, 1966, when this photograph was taken, there were nearly 320,000 American soldiers in Vietnam. In 1967, the Marine Corps had to resort to the draft for the first time, taking 19,000 draftees and increasing its presence to 78,000. At home, 50,000 demonstrators protested by surrounding the Pentagon; over half the population had no confidence in how the war was being handled.

WAR EFFORT

The Vietnam War showed that public support was essential for the continuation of a war in a time when television could bring events halfway around the world into everyone's home. It took years for the effect of public opinion to sway the administration, but in the end public antipathy to the Vietnam War meant that it was politically impossible to continue.

It is interesting to decide whether other wars in history would have continued if the press coverage had been as stark, unpartisan, and realistic. Before Vietnam, by and large the American people had supported its President and government in their decisions to involve the United States in open war. At home, during those wars, support was vocal and evident—to help fund the wars the public had backed the administration's war bonds and stamps; signatures of patriotism were collected, income tax rises were accepted without protest, and great energy was spent in ensuring a speedy victory.

The United States entered both World Wars unwillingly. When Woodrow Wilson took the country into World War I, he did so with a heavy heart, saying "It is a fearful thing to lead this great peaceful people into war...But the right is more precious than peace..."

One of the most important visible changes to the country at war was the absence of so many men of working age, and the involvement of so many women in work that would have been unthinkable before. War was the catalyst for the emancipation of women in the United States—the 19th Amendment, giving the right to vote to all American women, became law on August 26, 1920. Despite union pressure after both wars, the labor market changed forever thanks to the jobs women did during wartime.

There were, of course, other less beneficial results of war on the home front. In both wars, anti-German (and in World War II, anti-Japanese) sentiments led to violence. Anything—or anybody— that could detract from victory was suspect. This included conscientous objectors, sympathizers after the Russians and Germans made peace in 1917, and—in a move that was to have repercussions in postwar years—brewers, many of whom had German antecedents. Congress passed a prohibition law and amendment to the Constitution on January 29, 1919.

Right: American soldiers leaving Camp Dix, New Jersey, after the end of World War I in 1918.

Above: Women dancing during celebrations marking the end of the war.

Right: Advertisement showing a woman wearing a military uniform and holding a sign for war bonds. At her feet, a broom and a picnic basket full of household items. Photograph taken c. 1945.

Far Right: Film star Douglas Fairbanks (1883–1939) addresses a huge crowd in 1917 as he speaks for the purchase of Liberty Loans. These were government bonds sold to fund World War I. Eventually about sixty percent of the cost of the war was funded this way. Wartime America has always made good use of its Hollywood stars, both to summon up support and also to help morale.

Right: Americans take to the streets on hearing the news of Germany's unconditional surrender, May 8, 1945.

Below: Peace celebrations after the end of World War I, November 1918.

Far Right: An American lady encouraging people to sign the "Declaration of Patriotism" at the time of America's entry to the Great War, March 28, 1917.

PART 4

BUILDING AMERICA

CONSTRUCTION & BUILDING

By the turn of the twentieth century, America was a fast-developing country of cities and industries, when only a few decades earlier it had been a rural, agricultural country where a majority of its citizens lived and worked on the land. More people than ever were leaving their agricultural communities to work in the cities or in manufacturing, mining, and construction. In 1860 the numbers of people employed in these industries was a little over four million; by 1900 the figure was over eighteen million, and the United States was making almost one third of the manufactured goods in the world.

Capital investment in industry had similarly kept pace. America experienced a massive industrial expansion during the period between the Civil War and the start of World War II. This period saw the United States moving from a largely rural and agricultural economy based on self-sufficiency to an urban, industrial society where economies were built up on a framework of interdependency between the producers of foods and goods and those providing the services. This dramatic change in the economic and cultural landscape of the United States came about due to the increasing financial opportunities brought by advances in technology and mechanization.

Furthermore, the government poured money into the public sector to generate such growth, further enhanced by the transportation revolution and increased personal mobility, brought about by the railroads and motor cars, which increased accessibility to previously remote areas and enabled the transcontinental transportation of goods from one seaboard to the other. No longer did a particular product have to be made and consumed in the same general location. The proliferation of canals and roads extended the transportation network even further. In turn, this helped large-scale manufacturing to develop economically as heavy industry made the most of the new cross-country distribution systems.

Twentieth-century Americans discovered that they lived in a rich country, full of more natural resources than they had previously realized—not only plenty of good farmland, plenty of timber and gold

Previous Page: A group of construction workers labor above the streets of New York City as they work on the Empire State Building, 1931. The building was designed by the firm of Shreve, Lamb, and Harman, and took under two years to build. It was the tallest building in the world at 1,472 ft., a record it held until 1954.

Right: A group of Native Americans at work on a building site, c. 1935.

fields, as they already knew—but other mineral wealth such as oil, iron, lead, copper, manganese, and coal, and abundant natural resources such as rivers that could be harnessed to produce steam power and electricity. The exploitation of all this became possible with the use of cheap labor from the increasing numbers of immigrants desperately looking for work. In addition, the population of natural-born Americans was exploding. For such workers, living conditions were harsh and wages—especially for unskilled labor—were very low.

The ghettoes started to grow with the arrival of bitterly poor Irish escaping the famine at home, and the arrival in the Northern states of African-Americans escaping unemployment and starvation in the South. Both groups were prepared to work hard for barely adequate wages, and this in turn led to conflict with the native poor. To curb the spread of violence, the government passed legislation to improve employment conditions, and introduced the eight-hour work day.

Low taxes allowed living standards to rise after World War I, but for many blue-collar workers, life was still hard and employment precarious. Many low-paid jobs disappeared altogether after the Wall Street Crash started the Great Depression. The economy was on the slide and seemed irredeemably stuck until President Franklin D. Roosevelt

kick-started the economy again with his New Deal. For the first time, government stepped in to take a firm grasp of the economy. Jobs were created by instigating and part funding a huge nationwide public building and utilities program.

One of the biggest programs was the creation of the Tennessee Valley Authority (TVA) which broadly covered seven underdeveloped states sitting in the floodplain of the Tennessee River. The entire area desperately needed investment and the TVA set about building dams and hydroelectric plants to provide cheap electricity to attract new industry. The dams controlled the river flow and therefore flood control was established for the first time, enabling land to be reclaimed and either built on or put to forest. The scheme as a whole was the most successful of all the New Deal initiatives and dramatically raised living standards in those areas it covered.

During World War II, those men who did not join the services found jobs in the manufacturing industries—such as making armaments and airplanes—created by the wartime demands. As in Europe, women found employment filling jobs that were traditionally held by men. After the war, when the veterans returned, women were expected to return to their homes—not all of them wanted to—and many men found the womens' newfound independence and confidence disturbing.

Left: A group of boys overlooking the Homestead steel plant in Pittsburgh in 1903. The city's traditional steel and iron industries were, in time, replaced by service industries.

Far Left: The left hand of the Statue of Liberty under construction, c. 1884. Sixty men, not including its designer Frederic Bartholdi and his assistants, worked for almost ten years on the various parts of the statue. The 152 ft. high statue was designed and built in France, then shipped to America where it was assembled. It was dedicated in 1886, two years after this photograph was taken.

Below: The Wilson Dam under construction in Tennessee, c. 1923. This dam was an early part of the Tennessee Valley Authority plan, created by government inititative under President Roosevelt's "New Deal" to develop the Tennessee River basin—a huge area of some 40,000 square miles. The damming of the Tennessee and Cumberland rivers was to generate hydroelectric power as well as to control flooding and irrigation in the Tennessee Valley.

Left: Construction work on the site of a dam built by the Tennessee Valley Authority. This public corporation was in part developed to provide electricity to deprived areas of Tennessee, Kentucky, North Carolina, Virginia, Mississippi, Georgia, and Alabama, but also as part of a wider, more sociologically-ambitious project to regenerate the entire area by creating jobs and reviving the economy.

Above: The Hoover Dam on the Colorado River while still under construction. It took six years—from 1931 to 1936—to build. When finished, it stood 726 feet high and 1,244 feet across and contained 85 million yards of concrete. The reservoir it created stores nine square miles of water used for navigation, flood control, recreation, and irrigation, as well as for its main purpose of generating electricity.

Left: Steeplejacks removing the spiked crown from the head of the Statue of Liberty, on September 26, 1938, for renovation work before the World's Fair.

Right: A tire standing nine feet, six inches high and weighing 3,646 lbs. constructed for a giant earth mover to be used in the construction of airports and army camps. The factory was in Ohio, the U.S.'s leading rubber producer, in February 1942.

Below: The Tournalayer enabled the construction of low-cost concrete houses in just twenty-four hours. It provided an answer to a postwar housing shortage in America and Britan. The machine dropped a portable mold into which it poured concrete, allowing it to set before removing the framework. Pictured in the U.S., February 25, 1946.

Left: Elaborate stone carving of a kind now rarely practiced is incorporated in the construction of the Roman Catholic Church at 38th Street and Park Avenue in New York, c. 1956.

Far Left: One of the most dangerous occupations in America was that of the Blasters, who handled dynamite in quarries. Insurance companies would not issue life or accident insurance to these people. Photograph taken c. 1950.

Below: Hoover Dam near Las Vegas, Nevada, on the Colorado River in 1972. It is the biggest concrete dam in the United States as well as one of the biggest dams in the world. It straddles the Colorado River across the Arizona-Nevada border. The dam's name was changed to the Boulder Dam from 1933 to 1947 when President Herbert Hoover's stock was low. The name was restored by President Truman when Hoover's achievements were reassessed.

TOWNS & CITIES

The first truly modern city to be built in the United States was Chicago, Illinois. The famous fire of 1871 left much of the city devastated and cleared the way for the most innovative architecture yet seen to be built, including the first completely metal-framed skyscraper. This was the steel-skeletoned Tacoma Building (1890–94) designed by Holabird and Roche; other famous Chicago architects included Adler and Sullivan, into whose practice would come the master of U.S. architecture, Frank Lloyd Wright. Where Chicago led, other cities were quick to follow, and none faster than New York.

New York was originally a typical organically-grown sprawl of roads and buildings. But the city planners wanted a more logical and easy-to-use street plan. Most American cities were planned on a comprehensive and rigid grid system, but New York needed greater flexibility because of its topography. There the planners came up with twelve avenues running from north to south, each 100 ft. wide and numbered east to west. These avenues were bisected by 155 streets, each 60 ft. wide, running east to west. Each block was sub-divided into plots of about 25 ft. by 100 ft. Few open spaces were devised, as it was felt that the rivers were sufficient. However, activists lobbied for green space and Central Park, an area of 840 acres, was allocated in the center of the island of Manhattan. The plan was put into operation at the beginning of the twentieth century.

Cities on the east coast of the United States really started to grow in the mid-nineteenth century. All the major ports such as New York, Baltimore, Philadephia, and Boston were expanding rapidly with the influx of immigrants as well as with workers coming off the land and looking for jobs in industry. But already New York was outstripping its rivals. In 1860, Baltimore had 211,000 people, in contrast to New York's population of 800,000 and rising. However, the Midwest in turn also started rapid growth, especially Chicago, St. Louis, Detroit, Cincinnati, Milwaukee, and Cleveland. Many of these cities owed their growth to the agricultural trade and their position as markets for local

Right: Harmonica-playing steel workers perched high on a girder on the 22nd story of a building in the Murray Hill district of New York, c. 1955. The area is named after Robert Murray, whose wife plied British officers with conversation and refreshments long enough for American troops to gather for the Battle of Harlem. The area has long been—and is still—a highly sought-after address.

produce. Cities such as St Louis, Cincinnati, and Chicago acted as entry ports due to their waterfront positions. In 1860, Chicago had a population of 110,000, which lept to 300,000 only ten years later and to one million by the turn of the century.

In contrast, Southern cities were much smaller. The biggest was New Orleans with a population of just over 100,000 in 1850. At the same time, the other big cities of Richmond, Mobile, Louisville, Memphis, and Charleston had less than half that number. Furthermore, five Southern states had no town with more than 10,000 people. To grow into a city, an ambitious town needed to attract the railroads, which would bring people in numbers, along with a great deal of trade. The railroads, on the other hand, wanted to go to the centers where there was already business for them—and these tended to be the ports and main market centers.

The West was slow to develop large townships and cities, but as it became more accessible to American citizens and the new immigrants due to the railroads, the cities developed. In 1860, Denver was just a name; by 1900 it was a city of 134,000 people. Portland leapt from 800 people in 1850 to 200,000 by 1910. Seattle similarly shot up from 1,000 people in 1870 to 237,000 by 1910. This phenomenal growth was largely due to the influx of people and services prompted by the gold rushes in the Yukon and Alaska. Further south in California, Los Angeles had a population of 5,000 in 1870. Then the railroad arrived with two rival lines, the Southern Pacific and the Santa Fe, allowing cheap fares. This brought in thousands of migrants so that within thirty years the city's population topped 100,000.

Towns sprang up around the new-growth industries, particularly coal and steel. Pittsburgh was one such city, as were the Pennsylvania towns of Scranton, Wilkes-Barre, and Carbondale. The biggest visual change to American cities was the arrival of the skyscraper, mentioned at the start of this chapter. Tall buildings had been built in New York, but true skyscrapers had to await the technology to build them—steel skeletons, better concrete, better knowledge of construction and of loads and stress tolerances, but above all, the invention of the electric elevator to get people up and down the high buildings quickly. Another technological problem which had to be solved before skyscrapers became viable was the supply and disposal of water and sewage to the upper floors of high buildings. Once this was resolved and the first electric elevator demonstrated in 1889, buildings have soared upward in the U.S. ever since.

Left: A building in the course of construction on Van Buren Street, Chicago, September 30, 1894. It is being made fireproof by tiles around the steel frame. By this date, Chicago had transformed from an insignificant small town into an important railroad hub. Chicago became a city in 1837 and was connected to the East Coast by rail in 1852. Chicago rapidly expanded in the 1920s during Prohibition, at which time it became notorious for its gangsters and racketeers.

Far Left: The dome of the Capitol building, Washington D.C., under construction around the time President Abraham Lincoln took office in 1861. The building itself was designed in 1792 by William Thornton; the British burned the unfinished building in 1814 and it was not finally completed until 1827. The dome, designed by Thomas Walter, was added later. Washington had become the seat of Congress in 1800 after being chosen by George Washington as the legislative center of the United States.

Right: Workmen clinging to chains on a crane to reach the top of a skyscraper, seemingly unafraid of the height as they swing above the skyline in 1913. The tallest building in the world at this time was the Woolworth Building at 792 ft. It was dubbed the "eighth wonder of the world."

Below : A workman balancing on scaffolding, during the construction of the framework for the 150-foot aerial on top of a building in New Orleans, in 1925. New Orleans expanded rapidly in the twentieth century after vast deposits of oil and natural gas were discovered nearby.

Far Right: Skyscrapers in Manhattan, New York City, 1930. By this date the island already had a distinctive skyline of ever-growing skyscrapers. Manhattan was ideal for such huge buildings as its rocky terrain provided a good, solid foundation, but architects needed the latest technological developments in lightweight steel frames and the invention of the electric passenger elevator to make skyscrapers a practical reality.

Above: A worker pauses for a sandwich, resting on a girder during the construction of a New York skyscraper in 1930. At this date the Chrysler Building was the tallest building in New York City and the world at   seventy-seven stories and 1,046 ft. Interestingly, even though it was built by Walter P. Chrysler, the building was never owned by the Chrysler Corporation. The building's rule as tallest in the world lasted for only one year, as the Empire State Building shot up to 102 stories and 1,250 ft. The steel frame of the Empire State Building, weighing over 50,000 tons, was erected in an astonishing six months.

Right: A group portrait of construction workers standing among steel beams during the construction of the Empire State Building, 350 Fifth Avenue, New York City, 1931. These men assembled an astonishing four floors or more per week. It is built of limestone, granite, and aluminium, and stands 1,250 ft. tall to the top of the dirigible mooring mast. Amazingly, it came in under budget (at $41 million instead of the expected $60 million), as prices dropped during the Depression. The building was designed by Shreve, Lamb, & Harmon as offices but it was opened during the Depression and could only rent out forty-six percent of the offices—leading to its nickname of the "Empty State Building." The Empire State Building was the tallest building in the world for forty-two years.

Right: Cranes on a construction site in central Detroit, Michigan, c. 1955. Detroit became famous for it motor manufacturing industry. Ford, Chrysler, and General Motors all developed plants there.

Far Right: Construction of the Roman Catholic church at 38th Street and Park Avenue, in New York, c. 1956.

Left: Two construction workers on the Pan-American Building standing on girders fifty-nine stories above the New York streets, June 16, 1962.

Below: Construction workers completing Brooklyn Bridge, which spans the East River between Brooklyn and Manhattan. The bridge was originally opened in 1883 and was the first bridge to link Manhattan Island with the mainland. Before the bridge, people had to use ferries to cross the water. Brooklyn Bridge was designed by John Roeblingh, a German-American, but it was his son and daughter-in-law, who completed the project after his death in 1869. The bridge took fourteen years to build and was constructed by Americans and immigrants principally from Ireland, Germany, and Italy. The bridge cost $16 million and was the longest and highest bridge constructed anywhere in the nineteenth century.

Above: A section of a new concrete Dynacore being used at a site in Chicago. Its hollow construction makes it much lighter than conventional concrete. September 3, 1965.

Right: Construction work in progress on the new Madison Square Garden arena at New York City, November 29, 1966. The complex was designed for sports, concerts, entertainment, and other indoor events. The magnificent Penn Station was demolished in 1963 to make way for this vast leisure complex. Its destruction was the first time New Yorkers took real notice and protested about their disappearing architectural heritage. Since then the city has been much more careful to preserve its landmarks. The replacement Penn Station is hidden underground beneath Madison Square Garden. The porticoes on the right belong to the front of the General Post Office which was designed by the same architectural firm, McKim, Mead, & White, as designed the original Penn Station. Completed in 1913, across the top of the facade reads the words "Neither snow nor rain nor heat nor gloom of night stays these couriers from the swift completion of their appointed rounds."

RAILROADS

By the 1830s, the railroad had gained acceptance as the new mode of transportation for the age. The first American railroad was the Baltimore & Ohio, which opened for business in 1830. On Christmas Day of that same year, the South Carolina Railroad began passenger service on a six-mile stretch of track with a locomotive built in America (as opposed to being shipped over from Europe, as most other early locomotives were), *Best Friend of Charleston*, becoming in the process the first railroad in the nation to use steam power in regular service. Five of the six New England states had some rail mileage by 1838, and even states such as Kentucky and Indiana were projecting new lines. The railroads rapidly became important employers; at this time a single company could provide work for 36,000 workers.

Railroad construction was so rapid that by the late 1850s rail mileage in the United States was nearly equal to that of the rest of the world combined. By 1860, the total mileage was more than 30,000 miles, with much of the new construction in the Midwest, especially in Ohio, Indiana, and Illinois. Many of the new lines in these states were extensions of such Eastern lines as the New York Central, the Pennsylvania, the Erie, and the Baltimore & Ohio. This rapid western construction caused a shift in the total traffic flow from the north-south axis of the Ohio and Mississippi rivers to an east-west axis of trunk line railroads serving Eastern seaports.

When the Civil War erupted in 1861, it was the first conflict in which railroads had an important role. Both sides made massive troop and supply movements by rail during the war, and basic weaknesses in the Southern railroads contributed to the ultimate defeat of the Confederacy. The Northern railroads successfully bound the Northeast to the Midwest and helped win the Civil War.

The transcontinental railroad in North America became a reality on May 10, 1869, when the tracks of the Union Pacific joined those of the Central Pacific at Promontory Point, Utah. The joining of the two coasts was deemed of such importance that even its phenomenally high costs were considered necessary by Congress. However, even Congress could not afford to bankroll the endeavor in its entirety, so

Right: A Northern Pacific Railroad crew and their construction train, c. 1885. Note the cowcatcher on the front of the locomotive and the shape of the funnel—the appearance of American railroads was already changing from its European beginnings.

instead, investors were tempted by generous land grants along the proposed routes. Such lands were acquired by New York investors and other Eastern entrepreneurs—much to the disgust of Western businessmen who felt cut out of their own destiny.

The joining up of the railroad fulfilled dreams of spanning the continent that were spurred by settlement of the American West that dated back to at least 1845. Interest in a transcontinental railroad was heightened by the acquisition of Oregon (1846) and California (1848) and the subsequent gold rush. In 1853, Congress appropriated $150,000 to defray expenses of surveying feasible routes, but the question of the best one quickly became a matter of sectional controversy.

The new railroads were major economic factors in the growth of the U.S., and particularly in the West. For the first time, sending goods to market became cheap and easy, and businesses could service demand much further afield than was previously possible. In return, the railroad brought back new settlers, new machinery and goods, and brought intense competition between the towns and settlements to lobby for the railroad to come through their town. The railroad route was often the deciding factor as to which town developed into an important city and which remained a backwater, sometimes to this day.

Once the South left the Union, Congress pushed through the Pacific Railroad Act (July 1, 1862), which authorized Central Pacific to build eastward from San Francisco and Union Pacific to build westward from Omaha, Nebraska, via South Pass; the two were to join at the California-Nevada line. Each company was to receive 400 ft. of right-of-way through public (or 100 ft. through private) lands and ten alternate square mile sections of public

land for each mile of track laid. Loans of $16,000 to $48,000 per mile—depending on the grade of the terrain—were also available as a first mortgage on the railroad. In 1864, Congress doubled the land grant and made the financial subsidy a second loan on the property. Congress yet again amended the original legislation in 1866 to allow the Central Pacific to advance eastward until it met the Union Pacific, thereby turning the project into a construction race.

In the rush to be first, many railroad companies went bust due to the huge investment needed to create them and their immense running costs. The companies took out colossal loans to fund the building and were forced, as a consequence, to sell railroad stock indiscriminately with the promise of high returns. In actuality, most investors never got their money back, as many railroad owners had to raise such vast sums to build the railroad in the first place, that they were unable to service the debt. Consequently, they did little or no investing in the infrastructure, workmen were laid off, and lines stopped in the middle of nowhere. The Erie Railroad, the Northern Pacific, the Union Pacific and the Atchison, Topeka & Santa Fe all went bankrupt in 1893. The stakes were high and business was cutthroat; ticket prices were slashed to undercut the opposition, railroads went on different tracks to the same destination, and huge amounts of stock were sold. It couldn't last, and reason finally prevailed. By 1900, mergers had produced six distinct systems which put great efforts to structuring sensible schedules and realistic fares. America at last had a railroad system to be proud of. But with the advent of the combustion engine, the golden age of the railroad was over before the start of the 1920s.

Left: Garrison railroad station in 1859 looks like a scene from *High Noon*. The ferry service across the Hudson River to West Point and Cozzens is at right. All means possible were employed by ambitious town owners to get the railroad companies to build the tracks and the station at their stop. Bribery and corruption were the norm as the decision was literally make or break for rival settlements in the area.

Far Left: An early photograph of a railroad construction train, c. 1850.

Below: The U.S. transcontinental railway under construction in the snow, 1860.

Far Left: The Civil War was the first major conflict in which railroads played an important role. There was considerable infrastructure damage during the war years—this is the Northeastern Railroad Depot in Charleston, South Carolina, after it had fallen to Sherman's Union forces.

Left: The vastness of the continent and the enormity of the task of building the transcontinental railway is summed up in this 1866 photograph.

Below: Today, the wooden trestle bridges of the 1860s (this one was built in 1866) look particularly spindly and precarious. Indeed, many such collapsed under the weight of passing trains or in extreme weather.

Left: A Union Pacific construction crew, posing in front of a supply train, 1867. The Union Pacific railroad was involved in one of the earliest railroad corruption scandals. The construction company formed to build the railroad, Crédit Mobilier, charged almost three times the actual cost of construction so as to be able to award its handful of shareholders huge profits. Congress found out about the scam and proposed an investigation. To prevent such exposure of their practices and involve as many high-profile names as possible, the company then distributed stock to many influential Republican Congressmen. The fallout from the scandal was so great that even President Grant (who was not in office when the corruption took place and had no part in the cover-up) was made to look bad in relation to the matter.

Above: Steam locomotives on Devil's Gate Bridge in 1868 during construction of the Union Pacific Railroad, one of the two railroads forming the first transcontinental line in the U.S.

Left: Railroad construction crews were pushed hard. This is on the Southern Pacific line where, on April 29, 1869, ten miles of track were laid in a single day.

Above Right: The building of the railway bridge over the river at Salt Lake City in Utah in 1867, with the beginnings of a settlement by the Mormon sect evident.

Right: Archer, Wyoming, and in 1867 that meant one had to get off the tracks and travel by wagon.

Above: By 1868 the two railroads (Union and Central) were getting ever closer as construction continued apace. Here a Central Pacific crew lays track in Nevada.

Right: The great day dawned and crowds gathered. The railroads met at Promontory Point, Utah, and a golden spike was driven in to celebrate.

Above: May 10, 1869. After the Golden Spike had been driven in at Promontory Point, the locomotives of the Canadian Pacific and the Union Pacific Railroad met.

Right: A Union Pacific Railroad board meeting in 1868.

Overleaf: Railroad workers entertain visitors at a railroad camp alongside a construction route in South Dakota in 1889.

The heavy wartime traffic from 1941 through 1945 helped the railways recover from the hard times of the depression of the 1930s and to retire a major portion of their debt. The war years also saw women take over many jobs on the railroads.

Top: William Morrison, a fireman on the Chicago and Northwestern Railroad, lights his pipe, January 1943.

Above: Railroad yardmaster in his Hammond, Ohio office, January 1943.

Right: Female railroad mechanics in New York, February 10, 1942.

Above: Penn Station, along with its "sister" building, the U.S. General Post Office across the street, was the crowning glory in the careers of the architectural company McKim, Mead, and White. The many-columned building, completed in 1913 and home to the Pennsylvania Railroad, was based on the Roman Baths of Caracalla. Its destruction to make way for Madison Square Garden proved to be the catalyst for New York to establish the Landmarks Preservation Society. Many New Yorkers were rightly horrified when Penn Station was torn down in 1965 and have since fought tooth and nail to preserve the city's remaining architectural masterpieces, including the once-doomed Grand Central.

Far Left: Ramona Estrada at work on the Atchison, Topeka & Santa Fe Railroad locomotive shop in San Bernardino, California in March 1943. More commonly known as the Santa Fe Railway, this was one of the largest in the United States. Chartered in Kansas in 1859, it would later help in the settlement of the Southwest. Until 1920, the Santa Fe flourished and grew to more than 11,000 miles of track. By 1941 it had more than 13,000 miles of track.

Left: Crowds gather at the main information booth of Penn Station in 1955. A giant image of a railroad conductor looms over the concourse. Since the 1950s, the growth of commercial air travel and a huge increase in private automobile ownership has contributed to a substantial reduction in rail use.

The first modern road in America with a specially hardened surface was a sixty-six-mile turnpike, built in 1794, connecting Philadelphia with Lancaster, Pennsylvania. It proved a great success and quickly provided profits for the owners. Other interested parties were quick to notice these healthy profits, and over the next thirty years, a number of private companies were founded to build turnpikes. Such companies built over 4,000 miles of toll roads, mostly in New England and the states along the Eastern seaboard, where the majority of the U.S.'s commerce and money were found. Private finance was raised for such roads and tolls were charged for their use.

It did not take long for the state and local governments to notice the commercial benefits of having such a good communication with the outside world, and they, too, started to invest in roads. However, local jealousies and squabbling over funding rapidly ended state investment. After the mid-1830s, the desire for turnpikes subsided as the expense of their upkeep became apparent, and even honest citizens endeavored to avoid paying their tolls. Freight costs, too, were considered too high for the type of goods they carried, such as food and animal feed, and soon thousands of miles of road were abandoned and left to grow over.

The turnpikes had another unforeseen role. They helped thousands of pioneer families move their goods and chattels across America. Even cattlemen used the roads to herd their livestock to markets further afield. The largest of the turnpikes was the National Road, which ran across the Appalachians from Cumberland, Maryland, to end in Illinois, 834 miles away. This road in particular was used by thousands of migrants in their trek across the U.S.

The next big road building boom came in the 1920s and 1930s when the automobile came into wide personal ownership. New roads were built across the country as the motor industry hit the good times with auto sales at an ever-increasing high.

As in Europe, canals predated the railways. They were not so useful for moving people, but they were vital for moving heavy goods. The transportation of goods over water was a sound economic method of moving commodities from one place to another, but

Right: The "El," or Elevated Railway, which surfaces from New York's subway system for the last two miles of Broadway, seen in 1974. The El was built in 1870, predating the subway system. It was built to move thousands of daily commuters into and out of New York. Subsequently, other cities—most notably, Chicago—adopted a similar elevated steam railway system.

Above: New Yorkers stand on the shore near Macomb's Dam Bridge (Central Bridge), viewing the opening of the Harlem Ship Canal, June 17, 1895.

Left: Convicts in striped uniforms building roads near Atlanta, Georgia, c. 1870. Forced labor was an economic and socially useful way of constructing and repairing the highways.

existing watercourses did not always go in the desired direction and often contained hazards such as waterfalls and rapids. The answer lay in the construction of canals—often along the same level contours as the railways, which accounts for the proximity of their construction.

In 1816, there were only 100 miles of canals in the whole of America; as with the railways, these were almost entirely in the prosperous East. The waterway which really showed the way to the future was the Erie Canal, which opened in 1825, linking Buffalo on Lake Erie with Albany on the Hudson River—in other words, it connected New York to the Great Lakes and Midwest. The canal was 363 miles long and an engineering wonder with a total of eighty-three locks and eighteen aqueducts. It was so

successful and well-used that it had paid for itself within nine years, much quicker than projected. It had cut traveling time from twenty days to six and slashed freight charges from Buffalo via the Hudson River to New York. For example, shipping costs for a ton of wheat went from $100 to $10.

In fact, the canal was one of the critical factors which gave New York economic predominance through trade over the local rival ports of Boston, Baltimore, and Philadelphia, the latter having once been the most prosperous American city thanks to its position near the rich agricultural lands of Pennsylvania. By the mid-nineteenth century, New York—thanks largely to the economic prosperity brought about in the area by the canal—handled almost fifty percent of all foreign trade coming to the U.S. Primarily, it exported meat, cereals, timber, flour, and cotton from the South and imported foodstuffs and manufactured goods from abroad.

As with the turnpikes, entrepreneurs saw the opportunity to make big money. By 1840, there were 3,326 miles of canals built on investors' money at a cost of around $125 million. The canal building mania stopped after 1837 when, as with the

Below: The Brooklyn Bridge over the East River, New York, between the boroughs of Brooklyn and Manhattan—the two most densely populated areas of the city—shortly after its completion at which time it was the world's longest suspension bridge. The bridge was the work of German immigrant and engineer, John A. Roebling and his son Washington A. Roebling. Work started in 1866 and finished in 1883. The main span of the bridge is 1,595 ft. and the two spans on either side are 930 ft. each. However, John A. Roebling was also a wire manufacturer and he used steel wire cables in his bridge. Brooklyn Bridge was also the first to be built on pneumatic caissons.

Right: A road machine used to flatten tarmac roads in the 1920s. The use of asphalt for roads was developed in the 1880s.

Below Right: A Works Progress Administration (WPA) crew rebuilding the Morris Canal in New Jersey, c. 1936.

roads, the costs of running and maintaining the network on top of the original loans proved overwhelming. Few new canals were built after this date, as the system lost out to the bigger, quicker, and longer reach of the railroads. In common with the railroads, the road and canal systems were built on the hard labor of immigrants—broadly speaking, Irish immigrant labor in the East and Chinese immigrant labor in the West. Many poverty-stricken Irishmen, lacking education, money, or craft skills were forced into taking menial occupations which simply required brute strength and resilience. Conditions in the construction camps were atrocious. Sanitation was minimal; food was meager and basic. Accidents were frequent, and coupled with little or no medical care, many workers died unnecessarily, as well as through working accidents. To make matters even worse, the laborers were often cheated of their wages or had them docked unfairly.

Right: Workmen in a cradle working on girders of a bridge (the Golden Gate Bridge in San Francisco), c. 1936. The bridge spans a mile-wide strait between San Francisco and Marin County, which many engineers considered unbridgeable. Its designer, Joseph Strauss, proved everyone wrong. The Golden Gate was designed and built within four years and four months and opened for business in 1937. Its span was 4,200 ft. and it was the longest suspension bridge in the world for twenty-two years. At the midpoint it is 260 ft. above the waters below. One of the major concerns was to design the structure to withstand the 100-mph winds which whistle down the strait with alarming frequency, and to this end, it can swing up to 27 ft.

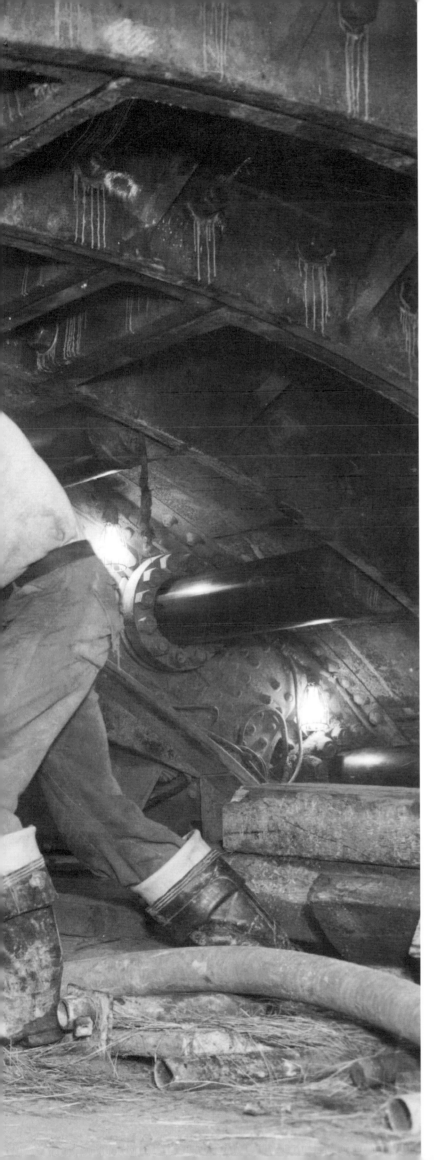

Above: A steel deck road under construction in Philadelphia, November 10, 1972.

Left: Construction workers, or sandhogs, working nearly seventy feet below the East River, New York, tightening the cast iron bolts lining the new East Side tunnel to Queens, c. 1955. Digging under the East River was hazardous and the tunnels difficult to build. The early East River tunnels were notorious for "blows" into the river when great quantities of compressed air exploded into the river with resulting loss of life. The annual death rate was a staggering twenty-six percent during construction of the early tunnels; this changed when the development and introduction of a medical airlock reduced the death rate to 1.5 percent annually. On one occasion, a tunneler is said to have been blown out into the East River, where he was recovered unharmed.

COMMUNICATIONS

Until the late nineteenth and early twentieth centuries and the advent of such technological marvels as the telephone and radio, communications in a country as vast as the United States was a problem. River systems and riverboats were important channels of communications, but until the advent of the electric telegraph, this was the only means of long-distance communication, although it was dangerous and expensive. The famous Pony Express was set up in 1860, but only survived thanks to a government subsidy. It could carry a message from coast to coast in ten days—better than the opposition, such as the Butterfield Overland Express, which used a more southerly route—but could not compete with new technology.

The first technological communications system arrived with the invention of the electric telegraph, which reached from coast to coast by 1862, following alongside the railroads. The importance of the telegraph was grasped immediately when, in 1844, Samuel Morse set up the first electronic telegraph between Washington and Baltimore. By 1878, the largest telegraph company, Western Union, owned 195,000 miles of telegraph and controlled eighty percent of the business.

As early as 1866, Cyrus W. Field had successfully financed the laying of a transatlantic cable. So, instead of news taking two weeks to get from New York to London by steamer, the telegraph could send the news instantly. This, in turn, had a dramatic effect on the stock markets and commodity prices on both sides of the Atlantic.

The telephone was invented and then perfected by Alexander Graham Bell. Although Scottish, he worked in America to produce the first telephone and was able to send his first message in March 1876. Realizing the importance of his invention, he and some associates set up the Bell Telephone Company. It rapidly became a success, and by 1897 the company had installed 56,000 telephones in fifty-five cities across America, including a link in the White House. Within three years this number had increased to almost 800,000.

In 1920, another main piece of the communications puzzle arrived. On November 2, the first broadcasting station in the U.S. opened in East Pittsburgh. The first national network—NBC—was created in 1926; by 1930, forty percent of U.S. households had a radio.

Today, in a world that has been shrunk in size by the Internet, mobile phones, satellites, and, of course, radio and television, the United States leads the way in communications.

Right: American mail vans in 1909.

Above: A mailman sits on a toboggan hitched to three dogs on the winter mail line of Lake Superior, c. 1870.

Above Left: A hastily constructed field telegraph station during the American Civil War. Men are up tree trunks being used as telegraph poles, April 1864.

Left: Men reading newspapers, seated on a circular granite bench at Herald Square, near 34th Street, New York City, 1899. By the turn of the century there were over 2,000 daily newspapers produced in the United States and a staggering 15,800 weeklies. Magazines also flourished, particularly after 1879 when Congress improved the postal rates for dispatch of printed matter. Until the advent of film, radio, and television, it was the printed word that informed Americans, and more of it was produced in the United States than anywhere else in the world.

Right: An exhaused newsboy sleeping on a stairway using a stack of newspapers as a pillow, 1912.

Above: A member of the New York Metropolitan police using a radio-telephone link for communicating with the city's police radio cars, c. 1930.

Left: Politician Huey Long (1893–1935) smiles while sitting behind several NBC microphones during a radio broadcast, c. 1930.

Right: Low-angle view of construction workers assembling the framework of the mooring mast of the Empire State Building in New York City, c. 1931. The mast was built to moor airships, signaling the freedom that this mode of transport and communication seemed to herald. In fact, as the photograph on page 299 so graphically shows, the airship was a chimera. It was fixed-wing aircraft that would dominate the skies, helped in 1925 when Congress began to subsidize mail carriage by air. Aviation was slow to take off in the United States, but by 1930 there were 50,000 miles of air routes over the United States, and the passenger figures were close to half a million, a pointer toward the importance of air travel to the nation today.

Top: Franklin D. Roosevelt, 32nd President of the United States, delivering one of his fireside chats to the nation in 1935. Roosevelt's mastery of radio showed the growing importance of electronic media in politics.

Above: Old signs being reclaimed by neon sign-making company Art-Craft Strauss. Many of their signs adorned New York's Times Square in 1950. The advertising industry may have its roots in Europe, but it was in the United States that it was developed and honed.

Right: A family sits in their living room watching a children's television program featuring a clown playing with a dinosaur puppet, 1955. Television is another 20th century invention that saw its main development in the United States. U.S. television programs dominate TV screens all over the world.

Above: A 1950s ice-cream soda store in small town Indiana has a television screen which brings in the kids, a feature of nearly every drug store in America.

Right: A technician prepares to wire together the components of the Bell System's Telstar experimental communications satellite, shortly before its launch into orbit, July 1962. Telstar was the first satellite to relay television programs between the United States and Europe. Satellite communications systems would change the way that the world communicated.

Far Right: Walter Cronkite reports during a live broadcast from the CBS News Control Center, Cape Canaveral, Florida, 1962. The importance of Cape Canaveral to spaceflight is massive. From here, the first American astronauts and satellites were launched into space. Its name was changed to Cape Kennedy by President Lyndon B. Johnson in 1963 to honor his recently assassinated predecessor. Subsequently, the name of the Cape reverted back to Canaveral in 1973, but NASA's Kennedy Space Center retains its name.

SPACE RACE

It was called the "Space Race" at first and started at the end of World War II when both the Russians and Americans vied with each other to see which of their captured German scientists would conquer space. Round One went to the Russians when *Sputnik* orbited the Earth. Russia also claimed Round Two when cosmonaut Yuri Gargarin was literally shot like a ballistic missile up into space and then back down again in a parabolic curve in *Vostock 1* on April 12, 1961. The Cold War was at its peak and the battle for who controlled space was fought with the implication that whoever was master of the skies would be master of the Earth.

Preparations and plans for getting into space had been drawn up by scientists and engineers for centuries, but technology needed time to catch up with ambition. By the early 1960s, the technology was making the dream possible, and in the U.S. the Mercury Program was started in order to get a man into space. Mercury developed a one-man spacecraft with a very basic life-support system, a retro-rocket with drag braking reentry, and parachute-retarded water-landing. The first American to leave the Earth's gravity was Alan Shepard on May 5, 1961, also shot on a ballistic trajectory. The first man to truly enter space and orbit the Earth was John Glenn on February 20, 1962 in *Friendship 7*. In total, the Mercury Program had two suborbital and four orbital flights.

By this time the stakes had been upped. President John F. Kennedy had vowed that the United States would place a man on the moon within the decade. The Gemini Program used a two-man crew system and developed orbital rendezvous and docking procedures—both important elements in a lunar landing program. Ten successful Gemini missions later, following a disastrous pad fire that killed astronauts Grissom, White (the first man to walk in space), and Chaffee, the first manned Apollo mission took place in October 1968. *Apollo 11*'s lunar module *Eagle* allowed Neil Armstrong and Edwin "Buzz" Aldrin to step down from the spacecraft to walk on the surface. Four more landings took place, the last by *Apollo 17* in December 1972. The space race had been well and truly won.

Right: *Freedom 7* and its pilot, Alan Shepard, would take a fifteen-minute ride in space on May 5, 1961.

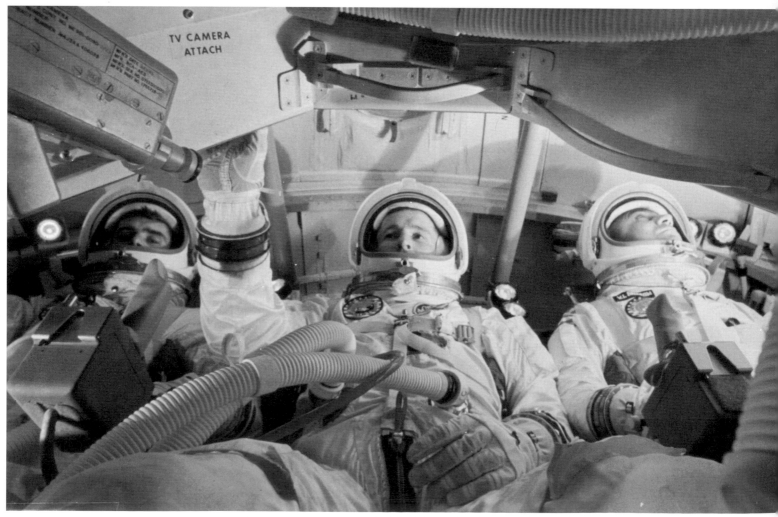

Opposite Page, Above: All would-be astronauts go through extremely rigorous training, including military survival courses. Initially, all astronauts came from a service background; they have proved themselves extremely capable of survival under difficult conditions—particularly the crew of *Apollo 13*. Lovell, Swigert, and Haise endured extreme conditions in their spacecraft following an explosion and the aborting of their mission to the moon.

Opposite Page, Below: The *Apollo* capsule housed three astronauts and the long time spent in space allowed plenty of TV airtime—until moon landings became so frequent as to be commonplace!

Left: Eleven other people have stood on the moon since Neil Armstrong's "small step for a man," the last two being Cernan and Schmitt from *Apollo 17*.

Below: Mission Control, Houston.

Left: Neil Armstrong and Stars and Stripes on the Sea of Tranquillity.

Right and Below: The *Apollo 11* astronauts in quarantine after their successful mission with President Richard Nixon. From left: Neil Armstrong, mission commander; Mike Collins, pilot of Command Module *Columbia*; "Buzz" Aldrin, pilot of Lunar Excursion Module *Eagle*. The crew splashed down in the Pacific and were picked up by helicopters from the aircraft carrier U.S.S. *Hornet*.

Above: *Apollo 14* crew was Alan Shepard (the first American in space was determined to set foot on the moon and did so at age 45); Stu Roosa, pilot of the Command Module; and Ed Mitchell (seen here beneath the mission logo), the pilot of the Lunar Excursion Module.

Right and Inset: *Apollo 14*'s mission included a long trip to the moon's Fra Mauro hills with a handcart. Future missions benefited from the Lunar Rover, a four-wheeled buggy. When *Apollo 17* said goodbye to the moon, NASA was working on plans to make the process of going into space cheaper and easier. The result was the Space Shuttle.

PART 5   LIVING IN AMERICA

CITIES & TOWNS

America made the big leap from being a largely rural-based agricultural country to an urban, generally mechanized country in the late nineteenth and early twentieth centuries. This was because many people left a hard life working on the land for better-paying jobs in the fast-growing cities and towns springing up around new industries.

With the growth of the cities, urban problems became more apparent—the large urban centers inevitably attracted immigrants and they naturally gathered together in ghettoes. Almost by definition, immigrants were poor and were forced to live, at least initially, in overcrowded, crime-ridden, and insanitary conditions; epidemics and disease were a constant threat. For example, in New York the Lower East Side had its tenement slums continuously occupied by the latest poverty-stricken immigrants. First the Irish arrived, then the Italians, and then Jewish immigrants. As they settled down and started to improve their prospects, they moved out of the tenements to a better living in the Bronx, Queens, and Brooklyn. Meanwhile, the latest poor immigrants moved in. Hostility toward the inhabitants was considerable and prompted calls for a cessation of immigration. Charitable groups worked to help immigrants assimilate into their new environment and for better standards of housing, education and fresh air in the parks.

Due to wholesale immigration, American towns grew faster in the first half of the nineteenth century than at any other time. At this stage, the built-up areas were mainly commercial centers rather than the manufacturing centers that they later became. The cities provided goods and services to the surrounding agricultural hinterlands and acted as the marketplace for forward distribution and sales.

The urban centers remained tightly concentrated with workers and inhabitants. But once the new rapid transit systems became established and reliable—principally the electric trolley and subway systems—it became possible for the white-collar city workers to escape from the city with all its squalor and teeming masses to a quieter, more civilized urban environment. By 1900 the suburbs of New York were home to over a million people—which was more than the city held itself. This spread of the suburbs only increased as the ownership of automobiles became possible for increasing numbers of people, allowing them to commute from greater distances to the city every day. This pattern was reproduced, albeit on a lesser scale, in towns and cities across America.

Changes in city life came thick and fast in the late nineteenth and early 20th centuries. One of the most obvious differences was the coming of electricity, which didn't just affect the transportation

Previous Page: The Fuller Building (designed by Daniel H. Burnham & Co. and completed in 1902) was originally named after its developer, but rapidly became better known as the Flatiron Building. The Flatiron—seen here in 1921—sits at 175 Fifth Avenue, and is twenty-one stories and 286 ft. high. Its unusual wedge shape is due to its triangular site. For many people, the Flatiron signifies the true start of the age of the skyscraper, with its early steel-case construction. It was the first self-sufficient skyscraper, with its own electric generator which provided all the heating and electricity. The building also incorporated a fire prevention system—fire being a particular hazard with tall buildings.

Above: Manhattan at night, as seen from the top of the Empire State Building in November 1946. Unusually for Manhattan, the skyline changed little during the period of World War II, due to the economy being diverted into war effort.

Left: Traffic on Fifth Avenue in Manhattan, New York, 1925. The private automobile was rapidly changing the nature of city streets, and the roads became increasingly congested as more and more people owned automobiles.

system; it also brought light to the streets. Gas lights, of course, already illuminated many of the bigger towns and cities, but the light they shed was more of a dim glow than actual illumination. The first town to properly light up was Cleveland—the home of the inventor of the electric arc lamp, Charles F. Brush—in 1879. Other towns and cities quickly copied the idea as the benefits of good lighting made citizens demand the installation of electricity. One important benefit was that it made the streets much safer from muggers and random violence, and in turn encouraged people to stay out late as well as allowing factories to operate around the clock. For the first time, nightlife for the masses became possible and entertainment and social amenities such as restaurants and theaters proliferated.

In the twentieth century, city inhabitants polarized: the poor lived trapped in ghettoes, while the rich lived nearby in luxury. What was missing were the reasonably affluent classes who moved out to the suburbs. In hard economic times, this tendency became even more pronounced: when poverty struck hard in the countryside, the poor moved into the big cities in their search for work where they were forced to live in the urban slums.

The economy as a whole expanded phenomenally during and after World War II. The rich inevitably got richer, but also far more people were sufficiently well off to afford their own homes, and as a consequence the suburbs exploded out ever further, often creating vast urban conurbations and making it hard for the stranger to tell where one city ended and the next began. This pattern continued throughout the second half of the twentiethth century and looks like continuing in the twenty-first century.

Above: Slum housing in New York occupied mainly by immigrants from South America, in the area known as "Hell's Kitchen" in Manhattan, May 1980. Hell's Kitchen is the area lying west of Sixth Avenue between 30th and 57th Streets, and until 1945 the area was notorious for criminal activity.

Right: Two children drinking root beer in Wilfred Allen's county store in Sudbury, Massachusetts, c. 1950. The store claims that this was the first soda fountain installed in New England, in 1881.

Top Left: View of a snow-covered downtown intersection (Market and North 13th Streets) with streetcars, automobile traffic, and pedestrians, in Philadelphia, Pennsylvania. Theater marquees and small businesses line the streets in this 1939 photograph.

Left: A merchant mariner by the East River in Lower Manhattan, New York, with the buildings of Wall Street behind him, c. 1947.

Above: A game of pool being played in a general store in Franklin, Georgia in 1941. Pool quickly earned a reputation for being a classic timewaster for young people.

Left: Children at play on the city streets; two young boys sit on the sidewalk, building a house of cards in 1907.

Right: A woman with a huge load of laundry in a New York laundromat, 1959. Many people living in small apartments did not have the money or space for modern conveniences like washing machines and instead had to use public facilities such as these. Nevertheless, the burden of washing and drying was considerably reduced by the availability of such useful amenities in cities and towns all over America.

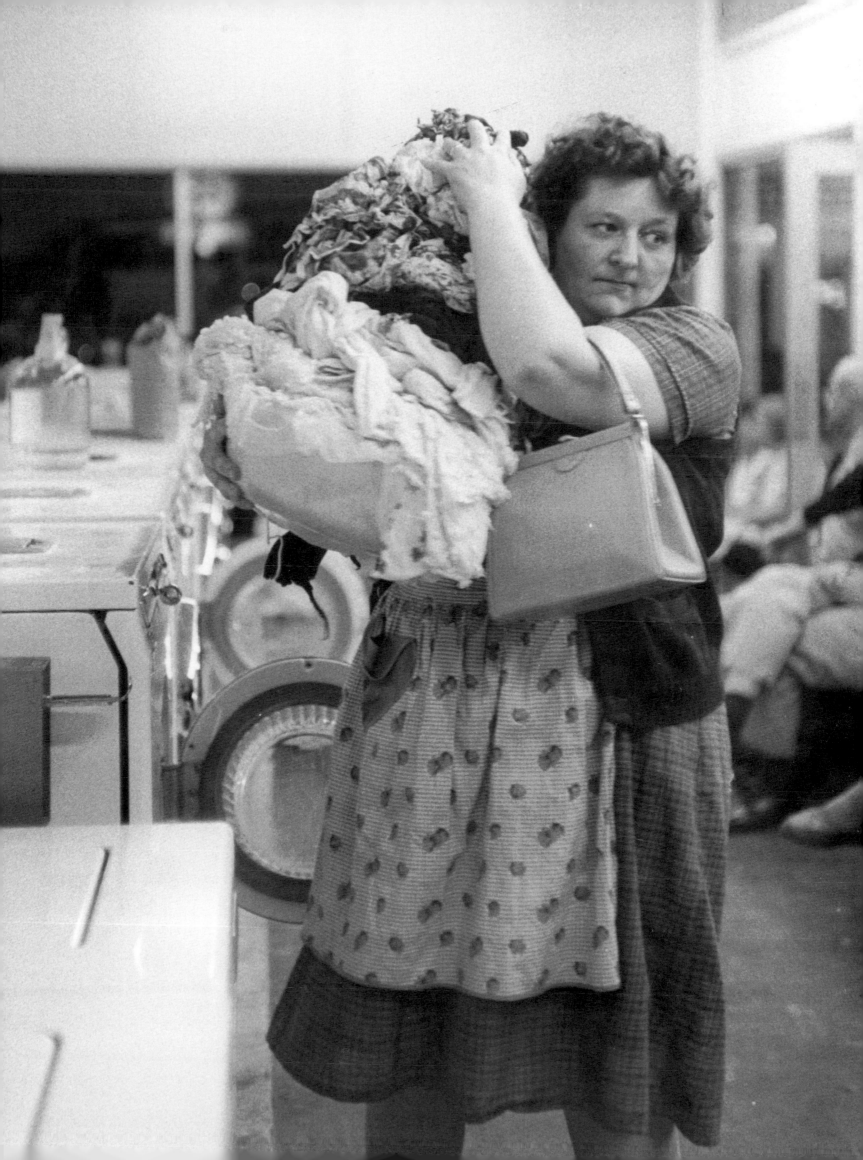

Above: Children standing in a barrel-filled alleyway in the Gotham Court tenement in New York City, c. 1890. Washing is strung between the tenements to dry. Scenes such as this were common in big immigrant cities, especially on the East Coast of America, where newly arrived immigrants crowded into insanitary conditions because they were too poor to move further away to find work.

Right: The Bowery, an Eastside thoroughfare in New York, was a notoriously rough area populated by thugs and lowlife of all descriptions. The name of the district comes from the Dutch *bouwerie*, meaning farm. Around 1900, the area was full of homeless people—many of them newly arrived immigrants—and bars. In 1884 there were an average of six bars per block, and a total of eighty-two bars. Unsurprisingly, twenty-seven percent of arrests in New York were made in the Bowery.

Left: A man nearing the top of an escalator bringing him up into Pennsylvania Railroad Station, New York, c. 1930.

Top Right: Lines of laundry drying between apartments on 138th and 139th Streets in the Bronx, New York, November 1936.

Below: Hester Street in New York's Lower East Side, c. 1890. The Lower East Side has traditionally been an immigrant area where newcomers from many different countries made their homes and each community established their own distinctive ethnic enclave—Jews, Russians, Italians, Irish, African-Americans, Germans, Chinese, and Latin-Americans.

Above: A group of boys rolling what they hope is New York's biggest snowball in Central Park, in the late 1950s.

Right: An American policeman standing in front of a wall covered with Chinese placards in San Francisco, c. 1930. The first Chinese came to the West Coast as fishermen and traders but the real influx came in the Gold Rush era and during the building of the railroads. The Chinese were widely resented and regarded with suspicion, to such a degree that they were legally excluded from entering the United States in 1882. By this time, however, more than 200,000 Chinese were living in the country. The Chinese exclusion laws were not repealed until 1943.

Far Right: Puerto Rican immigrants congregate on the stoop and in the street outside their tenement blocks in the most depressed areas of New York in 1955. The poorest parts of New York were once occupied by Irish, Jews, and Italians, but as they got better jobs and better pay, they moved out, to be replaced by the new poor.

RURAL LIFE

The 1860 census showed that five out of every six Americans lived a rural, agricultural life in the country, and the vast majority were of English, Scottish, Irish, or Welsh extraction; they were mostly Protestant and spoke English. All this had changed by the turn of the twentieth century. Freed from slavery, far more African-Americans were working the land, and the great waves of central European and Mediterranean immigrants brought many new faces and philosophies to agriculture.

America was a vast and still largely uncultivated land. Most of the best and richest lands were taken by the first settlers, leaving less desirable land for newcomers. But with the wholesale grabbing of Native American lands and general exploration of lands ever further west, new opportunities arose all the time. For example, when Oklahoma was opened up for settlement after the Native Americans had been thrown off the land in 1890, there was a scramble to claim the best areas.

The development of the canal and railroad systems in the middle of the 19th century enabled farmers for the first time to send their produce farther than the nearest towns to a wider internal market, and in time, from coast to coast. Always quick to catch on to a new source of income, farmers rapidly increased their productivity to make the most of these new opportunities and for fifty years or so, they enjoyed prosperity. But, as the farmers were able to make their produce more readily available in greater quantities, wholesale prices dropped, and by the turn of the century the good times were over for the farmers.

By 1900, the increasing mechanization of agriculture reduced the number of people working on the land—particularly in relation to preparing the land for crops and at harvest time. This trend only increased as the century progressed. Although there was still demand for unskilled labor in agriculture, the number of workers required continued to decline. Ironically, this loss of unskilled agricultural jobs through mechanization turned into a demand for unskilled urban workers in the newly mechanized industries. Many workers therefore left the land—not always unwillingly—for jobs in

Right: A large Cajun family on a farm near Crowley, Louisiana, October 1938. Like everyone else, agricultural families suffered during the Depression, although out in the country the effects were offset by the ability to grow food and raise stock.

Right: Ranchers at the Buena Vista Farm watching the harvest come in, 1890.

Below: A man fishing near the High Bridge over the Genesee River, near Rochester, New York, 1859.

Below Right: A rural family outside their sod hut on the treeless plains of Nebraska, near Coburg, 1887. Lands once occupied by Native Americans and buffalo were rapidly taken by settlers, many of old American stock from less-productive lands, but also by immigrants from north and central Europe—especially Germans, Scandinavians, Hungarians, and Poles.

the cities. The countryside depopulated quickly, and many small settlements all but disappeared.

However, the vastness and diversity of the United States meant that farmers in one region could be struggling while in another area they could be thriving. Regions which relied on a monoculture were particularly vulnerable to the vagaries of the climate, markets, and harvesting and distribution facilities. For example, the high plains of Kansas, the Dakotas, and Nebraska were settled by cattle-farming immigrants in the 1850s at a time when the region had unnaturally high rainfall that provided particularly lush pastures. As the climate reverted to its more usual aridity in the 1880s, farming there became much harder. Desperate farmers protested loudly, but to no avail. Then the dreadful, bitter winters of 1885-86 and 1886-87 destroyed many farming livelihoods altogether. Similarly, in California, traditional farming methods which relied on plentiful rainfall had to be abandoned in favor of much more arid agriculture and crops suited to the prevailing climate.

In the South, farming was a harsh life, even after the repeal of slavery. Cotton picking was hard and unmechanized until after World War II. Most poor Southern farmers, both black and white, lived from hand to mouth in a condition known as debt-slavery.

Above: A Native American camp in Nevada, May 1937.

Left: Chiricahua chief Goyathlay (1829–1909), better known as Geronimo, standing in a squash field with his family.

Right: Originally nomadic and matrilinear, Navajos support themselves by weaving and by making baskets and pots.

Following Page: Segregated shopping in the Southern states, c. 1925. Having won the right to freedom after the Civil War, many African-American families were without either education or land. They were forced to take work as sharecroppers, and sometimes even had no choice but to lease land and equipment from their former masters. The cost of this and housing rents were often so prohibitive that they were forced to part with much of their harvest as payment, leaving little or nothing to feed themselves and their families.

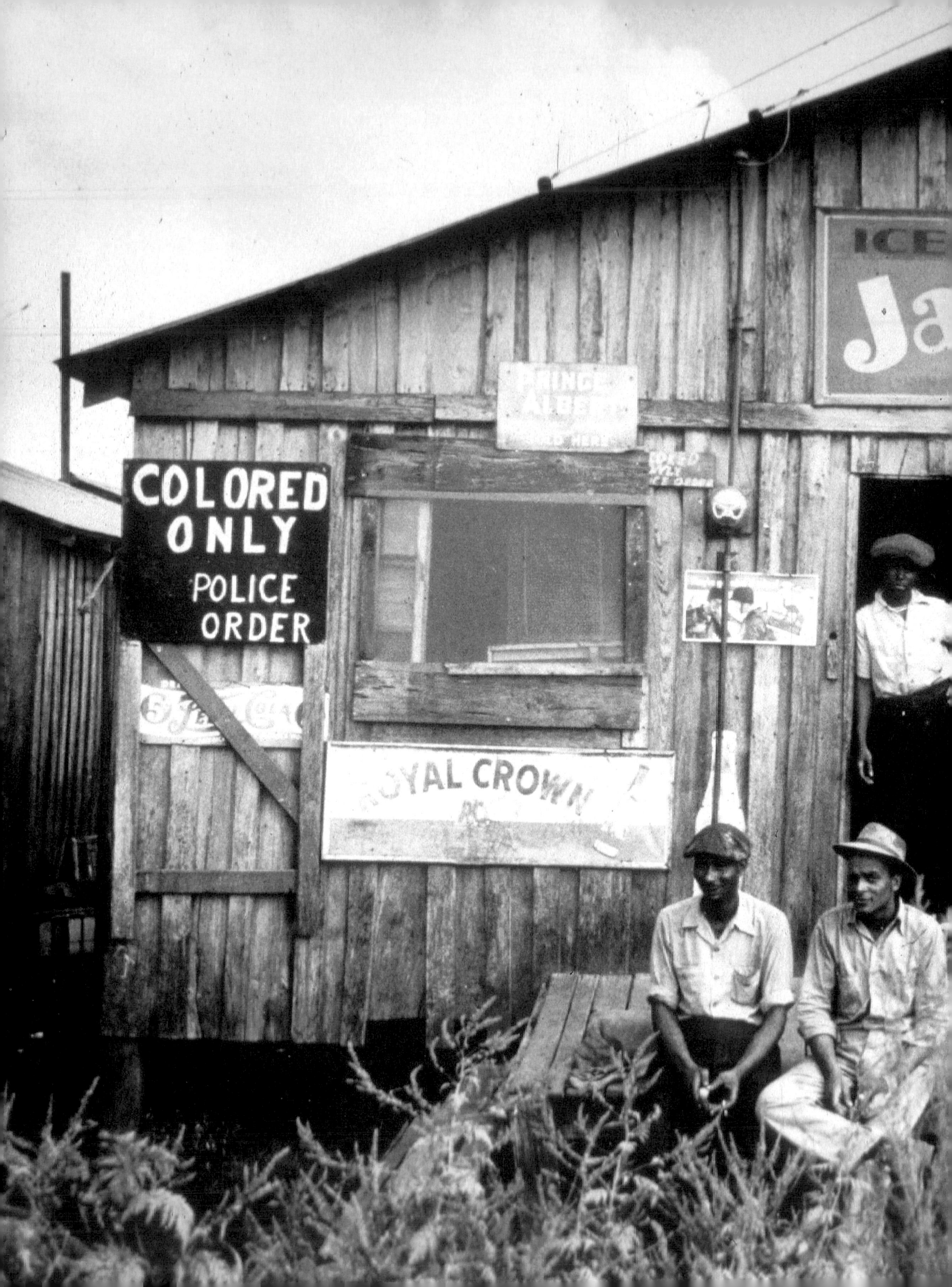
COLORED ONLY
POLICE ORDER
ROYAL CROWN
ICE

Left: A postman on his rounds accepts a welcome drink of water from some farm children, 1955.

Right: An elderly farmer in Tennessee reads instructions to a group of helpers who are leaning on their hoes, c. 1945.

Below: The strains of a harsh life clearly show on the faces of these agricultural laborers standing by their car in the Arkansas River bottom near Vian, Sequoyah County, Oklahoma, June 1939.

TRANSPORT

First there was the horse and wagon, the only sure way to move people and goods over the immense distances of North America. Then, as has already been seen, the advent of canals and railroads impacted the transportation systems of the eighteenth and nineteenth centuries, bringing urbanization around manufacturing points. As the cities grew into commercial centers, so new transportation problems arose—how to move the great numbers of people traveling to work in the downtown areas in the morning and back out to the suburbs in the evening. The first public mass-use urban transportation was by means of the horse-drawn omnibus. These ran on specified routes and schedules, but could only transport a few people at a time. Soon they could not cope with the ever-growing numbers of daily commuters. The next solution was the railway, but commuter railway systems were costly to build, dangerous and expensive to run, and not as practical inside the cities. They worked well in extending the suburbs, bringing workers into the city from farther away, but only a few cities, notably New York and Chicago, installed commuter systems inside city centers.

The turning point for urban mass transportation came with the invention of the electric dynamo, which eliminated the horse from the omnibus and opened the way for the trolley. The first successful streetcar operation started in Richmond, Virginia, in 1887 and was so widely copied in towns and cities across the country that within three years, fifty-one cities had built an overhead trolley system, and within ten years there were 15,000 miles of electric trolley lines in the United States.

Electrification also helped promote urban railways. Existing systems were electrified and a new answer to public transportation in congested cities became apparent—moving it underground. The first subway system was dug under the streets of Boston in 1897 and then New York in 1904. The answer to mass commuting into and out of big cities had been found.

Right: Pedestrian traffic, trolley cars, and horse-drawn carriages facing north on Broadway from 21st Street, New York City, c. 1895. Such public transportation was the only way to get about town until the arrival of the subway and the motor car just a few short years later. One great improvement, dating from the 1880s, was the start of a general trend to brick and asphalt the pavement. This made the roads cleaner and less potholed, as well as easier and faster for wheeled carriages to move along.

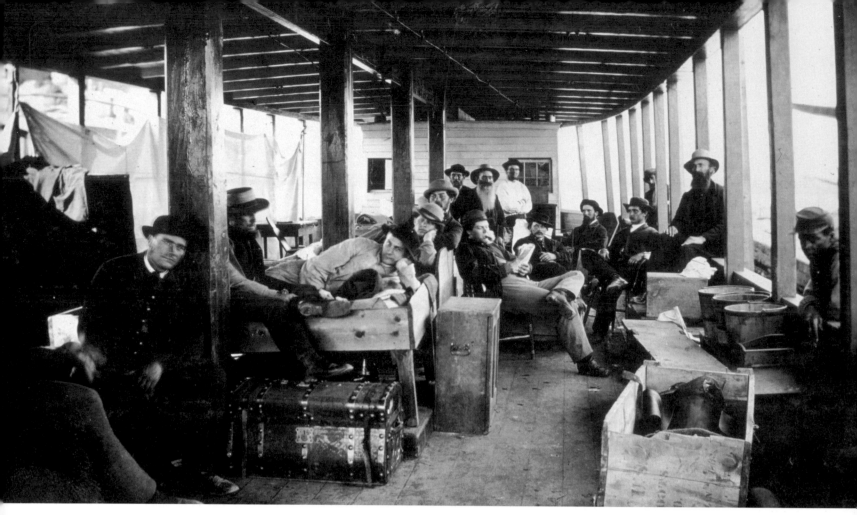

Above: Most people who came to America in the 19th century were used to traveling long distances—the voyage itself often being of epic proportions. Here, a group of travelers while away the long days at sea, sprawled between decks. Photograph dated 1862.

Right: A New York City winter scene around 1893. A man in a dark overcoat crosses a snowy Manhattan street as a horse-drawn trolley crosses in front of him. A sign on the front shows that it is en route for Harlem.

Opposite Page, Above: Men hanging from an overcrowded cable car on the Smith Street-Coney Island Avenue Line of the Coney Island–Brooklyn Railroad, en route to the Brighton Racetrack, New York City, c. 1897. The sheer weight of passenger numbers would force city governors to improve city transportation infrastructure at the turn of the 20th century.

Opposite Page, Below: Personal mobility became tangible in the first half of the twentieth century with the advent of mass-production. This is a 1930s photograph captioned, "A couple on a Californian beach proudly show off to the camera their new motorcycle and sidecar."

The United States is the spiritual home of the automobile, even if its actual genesis was in Europe. Americans have had a continuing love affair with their favorite mode of transportation ever since it first graced the highways. By the 1920s, the motor car was rolling off the assembly line in such numbers that it became an accessible form of personal transportation for many. Cheap credit made the financing of a family car possible—installment buying was heavily promoted by both Ford and General Motors as they did all they could to capture new customers. Such mass-market success rapidly catapulted automobile manufacturers into the top ranks of the national economy. By 1929 the automobile industry was the largest in the country and employed nearly half a million workers in Detroit, itself now the fourth-largest city in the U.S.

In 1920 just under two million cars rolled off the production lines; by 1929 this number had reached 4.5 million. That year, almost twenty-seven million cars, trucks, and buses were registered. The more cars, the more roads were needed and clearly Congress could no longer rely on private construction. Federal and state government had to find the funds and have a say in such a vital infrastructure. In response, Congress passed the Federal Highway Act in 1921 which provided fifty percent federal funding for new highways. The open road was the future of America, and the country grasped it with both hands.

Above: By the time this photograph was taken in 1935, anyone who was anyone had a flashy automobile. Here flamboyant film director Raoul Walsh (former assistant to D. W. Griffith) surveys his luxury car complete with white-walled tires. He is wearing his trademark—a black eyepatch.

Left: A scene that was to become familiar all over the United States—this is a 1935 parking lot that stretches as far as the eye can see.

Right: Almost as soon as the car was invented, so was the traffic jam. This is a c. 1935 aerial view of traffic congestion at the entrance to New York's Holland Tunnel. Cheap motoring allowed even poor people to own a car, and for the first time they could travel in search of work. In fact, many people drove all the way to California and the West Coast in general in search of a better life. They didn't always find it: the dark side of the automobile was the death toll on the roads which soared in the wake of increasing numbers of cars. In 1925, 25,000 people were killed directly due to the motor car, some 17,500 of these being innocent pedestrians who were luckless enough to get in the way. Drivers were still largely self-taught and pedestrians unused to the speed of oncoming traffic.

Top: Two women stand in the doorway of a Covered Wagon Company '37 Deluxe trailer parked in a sylvan setting in 1937. Touring with a trailer became a fashionable way to vacation and enjoy the wilder areas of the country with all the conveniences of home.

Above: It's bumper to bumper all the way along Fifth Avenue near 59th Street in Manhattan, c. 1941. By the middle of the 20th century, the automobile had made a huge impact on the face of urban America. The trolleys and cable cars practically disappeared to be replaced by gasoline-driven buses and automobiles. Rush hour has slowed to a snail's pace, and pollution levels are beginning to cause concern.

Right: Enter the bus. Another competitor to the railways, long-distance bus networks were cheaper to run once the highways were built. Here is a 1940 view of passengers boarding a New York Limited bus at a depot. A porter carries one of the passenger's suitcases while the driver stands by the door of the bus.

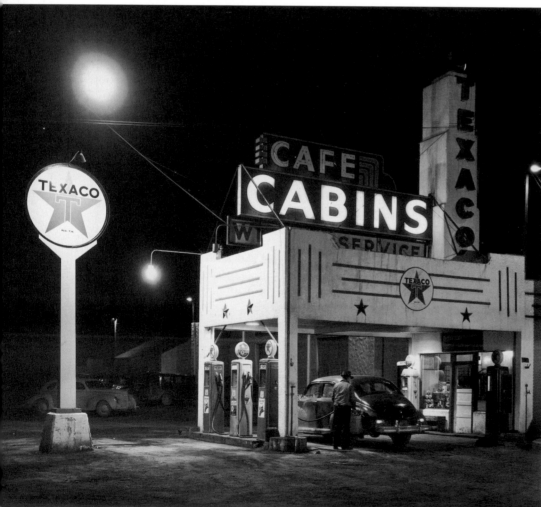

Above: Social life began to revolve around the automobile. Here, two couples ride in a yellow jeepster through Central Park, New York, c. 1940.

Left: It's wartime—1945—but gas is still cheap and plentiful. All over the United States, filling stations have sprung up, with local amenities from cafes to motels. Here, in Wendover, Utah, the neon signs advertise a cafe and overnight cabins.

Right: A young couple kissing in the front seat of a convertible, c. 1945.

Opposite Page: One of the truly great American inventions—the school bus. Here a Connecticut mother waves her daughter off to school, c. 1950. At first horse-drawn carts were used—by 1910, thirty states had pupil transportation programs in place. The arrival of the gasoline-powered engine saw the arrival of the school bus. Today, statistics produced by the National Association of State Directors of Pupil Transportation Services identify that there are 450,000 public school buses in the United States transporting some twenty-four million students around four billion miles daily.

Above: A group of women, dubbed the "Motor Maids of America," sit astride their motorcycles outside the shop they use as their headquarters, c. 1950.

Left: Postman Arthur LeBlanc from Berlin, New Hampshire, delivering post from his horse-drawn sled. This was the only way to get the mail through when the snow came down in the countryside, c. 1950.

Right: A drive-in cafe in Beverly Hills, California, in 1952. The drive-in is a way of life in North America—from banking to fast food, almost every service imaginable is available to the driver.

Below Right: Cars parked in a pickup bay at Northlands shopping complex, Detroit, Michigan, c. 1955.

Far Right: A busy motorway linking the Hollywood and Ventura freeways in Los Angeles, California, c. 1955.

SHOPPING

Shopping has always been a necessity for those who do not grow all their own food and are reliant on others for goods and services. In the past, shopping for fun—for luxuries and nonessentials—was always the prerogative of the wealthy, as most people had little income to dispose of after clothing, feeding, and housing themselves and their families. The revolution in the way we shop, and what we shop for, has its roots in the nineteenth century. Increased disposable income, mass-production techniques, and abundant mineral resources soon saw a consumer boom. Today's high streets boast shops, supermarkets, malls, products, and a level of individual choice that would be the envy of all previous generations.

Throughout rural America in the nineteenth century and for much of the twentieth century as well, the local store was invaluable. It would sell all household necessities, and the good stores contained much more. As the number of products available on the market grew, specialization took place and the number of outlets increased. Improved public transportation systems, especially for those living in or near a big city, meant that it was quicker to get to the shops. Now it became easy, economic, and fun to travel right into the heart of town to marvel at the city stores. The big attraction was the latest idea in shopping—the department store, which did what the local store had done, only better, by putting all kinds of goods under one roof. Some of the biggest names in retailing appeared with the emergence of the department store—among them Macy's in New York, Wanamaker's in Philadelphia, and Marshall Field in Chicago.

Another feature of American shopping was the development of the chain store, the first and biggest of which was the Great Atlantic & Pacific Tea Company, founded in New York in 1858; by 1915 the chain had over a thousand branches. Another successful venture was started by Frank Winfield Woolworth, who opened his first store in Lancaster, Pennsylvania, in 1879. By 1911 he could claim over a thousand "five and ten cent stores" all over small-town America. Woolworth made so much money that in 1913 the Woolworth Building on Broadway in New York City was opened as the headquarters of his chain of stores—it was built and paid for in cash and was the tallest building in the world until 1930. Chain stores became an essential part of the city scenery, selling everything from household goods to candy, clothing, toys, and medicine.

Right: The general store and post office on a Native American reservation in Ruidoso, New Mexico, c. 1885.

Right: Shoppers crowd around the bargain counters of the Siegal-Cooper Company's "The Big Store," located on the east side of Sixth Avenue between eighteenth and nineteenth Streets, New York City, 1897.

Below: A New York pushcart vendor selling fresh fruit, c. 1915.

Far Right: People lining up to buy coal during a coal strike, 1902.

Meanwhile, for people living in remoter areas, such excitement was impossible; the best they could hope for was the occasional traveling salesman, and the local country store was all they could patronize regularly. Then, a former traveling salesman, Aaron Montgomery Ward, realized that he could sell direct to his customers through the mail, and that by buying in quantity he could offer goods at a discount and still make a profit by cutting out the middlemen. Ward opened the first successful mail-order business in 1872 in Chicago. It had become possible for him and his imitators to deliver goods reliably and economically to remote areas in the 1870s, thanks to the new railroads.

Another Chicago firm became Ward's chief rival: Sears, Roebuck and Company opened for business in 1886. In 1890, they began to publish an annual catalog offering the widest possible variety of goods and merchandise. However, the real upturn in the mail-order business came thanks to the Post Office, which started free rural delivery in 1896. This cracked open the opportunity to sell goods through the mail, and catalog shopping became a real life-saver for rural dwellers.

Above: Patrons inside a dime store selling candy and various dried goods, c. 1930.

Left: The local store was often the center of the community. Here, a group of men sitting out on the porch of a country store on a dirt road in Gordonton, North Carolina, July 1939.

Right: Ethel Oxley proudly stands in her drugstore on the main street of Southington, Connecticut, in May 1942. Every inch of space is occupied with all manner of tempting goods—note the selection of Cuban cigars on the counter, no longer available in the United States since trade with Cuba was stopped during the Cuban Missile Crisis of 1962.

Following Page: Two girls buy a "10,000-Calorie Sundae" ice cream from Blair Parson's store in Lynchburg, Virginia, c. 1950.

Left: A woman shopping at an all-night store, c. 1950. Such convenience stores were the precursors to the big supermarkets which all but swept away small personal-service shops in favor of huge self-service stores.

Right: Ted Hustead's drugstore in Wall, South Dakota, which sells souvenirs of the Badlands to tourists, November 1950.

Below: Street vendors selling pretzels and hot dogs in New York in December 1975. The original "fast food" street vendors provided an invaluable service for those who wanted to eat on the move.

RELIGION

Religion and culture were inextricably linked together in the early days of America. For many immigrants, religious practice was a reassuring piece of home in a new and strange land. Often, it was through religion and places of worship that ethnic communities were organized. This gave the religious hierarchies a political strength beyond the strictly numerical complement of their officers. The prime example of this is the importance of the Catholic Church in the organization of, and influence over, the Irish community. The church oversaw much more than just the spiritual well-being of its parishioners; it also organized social functions, lobbied politicians and councils, and raised funding for a wide variety of causes—spiritual, moral, and communal.

Many of the earliest immigrants to America were religious outcasts seeking freedom of worship and thought in a new and spiritually unregulated land. The French settlers brought Catholicism (as did the British to Maryland), while the British settlers established various forms of Protestantism—there were Presbyterian, Episcopalian, Baptist, Lutheran, Methodist, and Congregational churches. Despite the ban on their settlement, a few small groups of Jewish settlers also arrived with their religious practices.

Traditionally, the United States has given a home to many and various fringe religions which were able to flourish in relative isolation (should they wish, and many did) from the rest of the mainstream community. Unconventional religious observance was very popular in the nineteenth century with groups such as the Shakers of Pennsylvania, the Mormons of Utah, and the Amish of New England. With the notable exception of the Mormons, most of these groups were short-lived and small in number—for example, the Shakers in their heyday between 1830 and 1860 had about 6,000 members.

In spite of the fact that many of these groups had fled religious discrimination in Europe, tolerance toward other religions was markedly lacking, and frequently resulted in open fighting, especially between 1830 and 1860, a particular era of dissent. Furthermore, within the different sects there was often quite vicious debate, resulting in frequent splits and factions.

Right: Evangelist Billy Graham shaking hands with admirers, c. 1966. He continued the tradition of popular evangelism at mass rallies around the country where the participants were urged to confess their sins and repent the ways of the devil. The most important Protestant groups in nineteenth century America were Baptist, Methodist, and Presbyterian, although by the turn of the twentieth century the Presbyterian church had lost ground to the two former groups.

Many of the more austere Protestant sects were spiritually led by itinerant preachers, especially in the far-flung West. Preachers set out with a horse and a Bible and little else but their passionate mission to convert and spread the word of God into a spiritually empty land.

Around the turn of the twentieth century other ethnic communitites started to arrive, bringing with them their religious observance. Asian immigrants brought Hinduism, Islam, and Sikhism, and the Eastern Europeans brought Greek and Russian Orthodoxy. Increasing numbers of Jews fleeing persecution brought Judaism. As these immigrant groups slowly assimilated into American society as a whole and the ecumenical movement gained momentum, people eased into a much more tolerant attitude toward other forms of worship.

Below Left: Mormon leader Brigham Young, second from left, with his colleagues, c. 1860. The Church of Jesus Christ of Latter Day Saints was formed in the late 1820s by Joseph Smith, who claimed angelic visions as his inspiration. He took his followers to Illinois but was assassinated in 1844 by local people. Smith was succeeded by Brigham Young, who took his 4,000 followers from Nauvoo, Illinois, to settle in Utah in the Great Salt Lake Valley. There they intended to establish their own state of Deseret, but because of the aftereffects of the Mexican War the area became part of Utah and therefore, of the United States. However, Brigham Young was appointed territorial governor and ran the area virtually as a private fiefdom.

Far Left: Mormons gathered outside a jeweler's shop in Salt Lake City, Utah, c. 1869.

Below: Evangelist Dwight Lymon Moody (1837–1899) with a group of orphans at one of his Chicago missions, c. 1870. All the churches became interested in education as a means of gaining more members, as well as educating the needy out of poverty.

Above: A young Mennonite boy in his traditional dress. Lancaster, Pennsylvania, March 1942.

Above Right: A rabbi photographed near Windsor Locks, Connecticut, in August 1942.

Left: A member of the Salvation Army in San Francisco, California, April 1939.

Right: Amish boys are easily identified by their distinctive hats and trousers. The Amish are of Dutch descent, and pride themselves on leading a simple life with simple pleasures. They live in the areas south of Washington D.C., and dress and live exactly as their ancestors did when they fled Europe in the early 18th century. Here the community is enjoying a day at the fair, c. 1950.

Right: An evicted sharecropper reading the Bible. Butler County, Missouri, November 1939.

Below Right: A young Jewish man holds a prayer shawl over his head before praying in a Rosh Hashanah ceremony at Yeshivah University, New York. c. 1950.

Far Right: Two smartly-dressed women leaving the Abyssinian Baptist Church in Harlem, New York, on Easter Sunday, April 26, 1943.

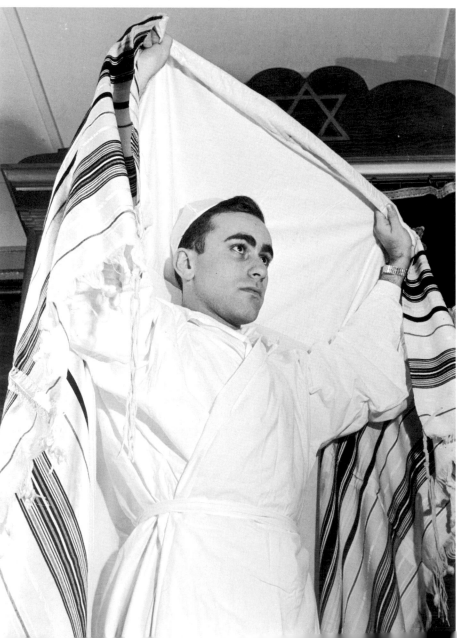

Above: A migrant worker reads a gospel pamphlet, c. 1954. He is lucky; most other migrant workers are unschooled and illiterate.

Right: Members of the Archdiocesan Sisters' Orchestra in concert at Symphony Hall in Boston on the 150th anniversary of the Boston See, March 29, 1958. Catholicism was not widely followed in the United States until the middle of the 19th century, when huge numbers of German and Irish immigrants gave the church a real representation. By 1870 there were seven million Catholics in fifty-five dioceses, looked after by 7,000 priests; this steadily increased until by 1921 there were twenty million Catholics, over a hundred dioceses, and 20,000 priests.

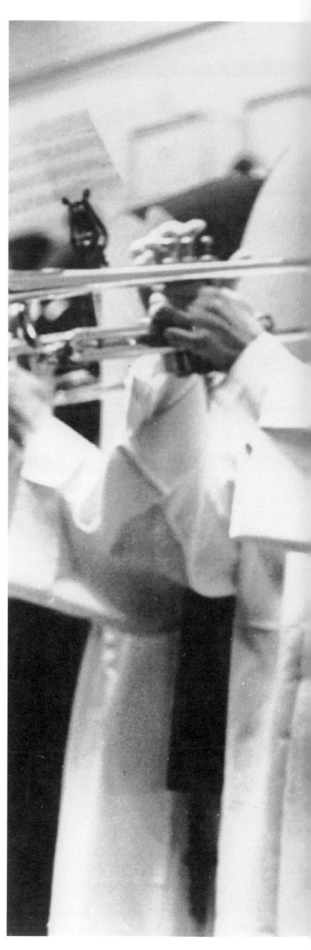

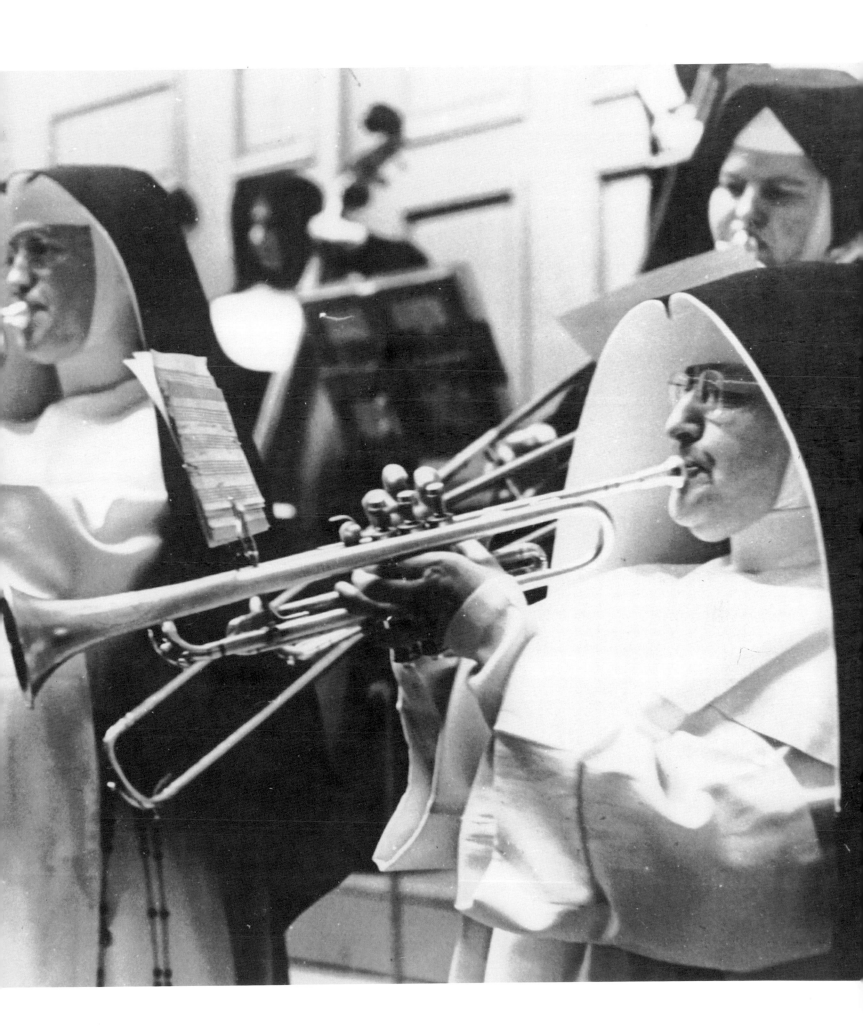

Above: People leaning over barriers to catch a glimpse of Pope John Paul II as he drives through New York to the U.N. Building, October 5, 1965.

Left: Friar Capistran Ferrito plays baseball with boys from Harlem, New York City, June 19, 1966. The Catholic Church, in common with most of the mainstream religions, likes to be closely involved with community problems where it can play an active role in improving local living conditions and act as an interface with the larger non-Catholic community.

Right: A member of the congregation wears a "Keep the Faith, Baby" sash to an African-American church meeting, 1967.

DISASTERS

Accidents happen in even the best-ordered society, and when they become national news, with photographs on the front of all the papers, they tend to be on a large scale. Many of the disasters in this section are caused by natural events—hurricanes, tornadoes, volcanoes, or earthquakes, with causes beyond human control. There are, however, all too many of the man-made variety, often involving transportation. These always seem so much worse because they appear preventable, and doubly tragic for being an accident.

In the front line of most accidents or disasters are the nation's firefighters and emergency services, who lay their lives on the line to save others. Until well into the twentieth century, devastating fires regularly swept through towns and cities, leaving the helpless and homeless in their wake. Often, local town councillors and city authorities took bribes from landlords to turn a blind eye to the risk of fire in slums and tenement dwellings. It usually took a tragedy of huge proportions to get the attention of the authorities and legislation moving. One such notable event was the fire which broke out on March 25, 1911, in the Triangle Shirtwaist Company, a New York sweat shop near Washington Square. Of the workforce of 500 garment workers, mostly young immigrant women, 146 died of suffocation trapped in their barred and bolted workplace. The outcry was so great that a state law was passed to improve fire prevention and to provide metal fire escapes.

Firefighters were originally unpaid, but the immeasurable value of a dedicated fire service was quickly apparent, and the Municipal Fire Department in Boston had the first paid professional firefighters as early as 1678. When the alarm was raised, firefighters used wooden rattles, bells, and drums to warn the townsfolk of fire. Until the mid-nineteenth century, fire engines had to be pulled by hand over the muddy streets. When they got to the fire, the water was in wells fifteen to twenty feet underground and every drop had to be pumped up to the surface and onto the fire by sheer muscle power. Firefighting became much easier when horses were employed to pull the equipment and to bring the water to street level. When motorized equipment arrived, the firefighters were able to save their energy for fighting the fire itself.

Right: Rail tends to be the safest regular form of transportation and accidents are not rare, but rarely fatal. Here, two trains have collided on an elevated track in New York City, c. 1920.

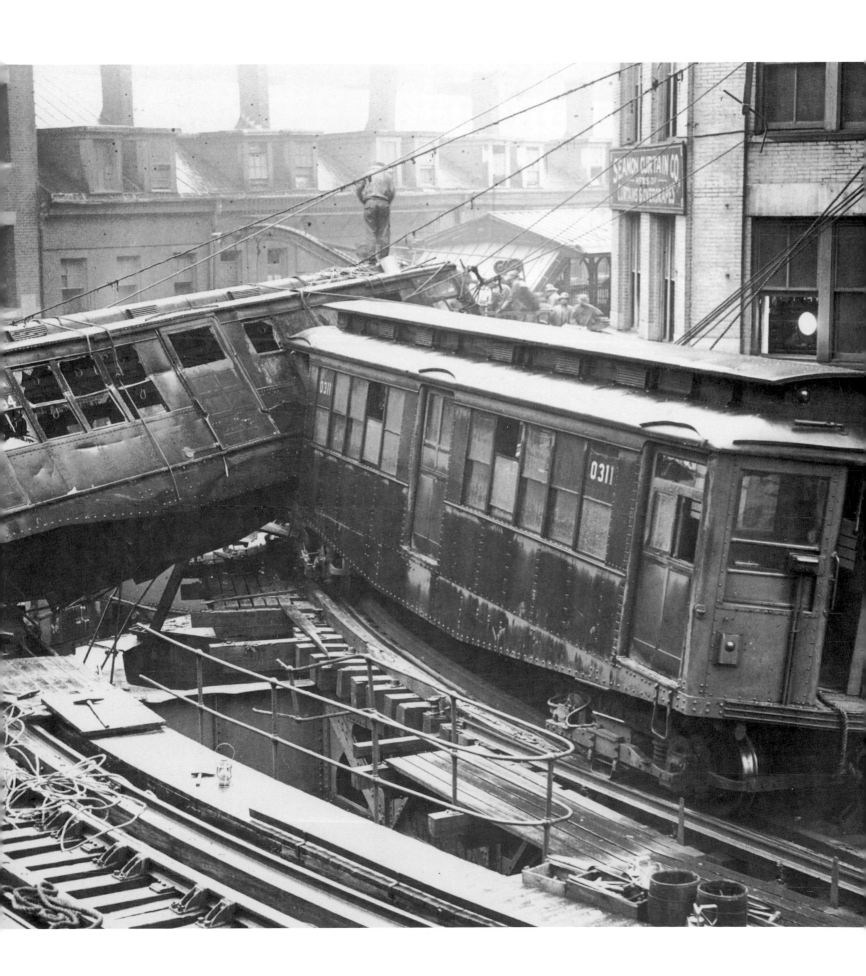

Above Left: War is the worst of all disasters and civil war the worst type of war. Here, members of the U.S. Christian Commission are seen at a Union camp near Germantown, Maryland, in September 1863. The commission, founded by the YMCA, helped regimental chaplains and provided small comforts for the troops. At this time there was little understanding of the mental effects of the experience of war and people who would be hospitalized in the present day, in previous generations were accused of "lacking moral fiber."

Left: A hastily-built railway bridge collapses in Maryland, c. 1890. Unfortunately, this was an all-too-frequent occurrence during the explosion of railway building across America.

Above: The worst natural disasters to affect the United States are those that take place in densely-packed cities, and the earthquakes that happen on the West Coast around San Francisco and Los Angeles have proved deadly. This is a photograph taken on May 19, 1906, showing the destruction caused to the main shopping area in San Francisco by the great earthquake. In the background is Telegraph Hill.

Left: Another view of the aftermath of the 1906 San Francisco earthquake.

Far Left: A salvage team attempts to recover the wreckage of the stricken steamship *General Slocum*, which caught fire during a pleasure cruise on New York City's East River. The disaster, in June 1904, resulted in the loss of over 1,100 lives.

Below Left: A woman helps to prepare food at an open-air canteen, set up following the 1906 San Francisco earthquake.

Below: The German airship *Hindenburg* (LZ-129) falling to the ground in flames after turning into a fireball while attempting to land at Lakehurst, New Jersey, May 6, 1937. The *Hindenburg* had been built a year earlier by the German government for the transportation in grand style of seventy-two passengers. It made sixty-three successful flights—many across the Atlantic—before this awful disaster. Its rigid frame construction burst into flame after a successful Atlantic crossing, probably due to hydrogen leaks being ignited by atmospheric electricity.

Above: A crowd gathered around the wreckage of Lincoln Beachey's crashed airplane, at Ascot Park, Los Angeles, California, February 14, 1914. While air disasters are less frequent than with other methods of transportation, they are more likely to be fatal. The United States has seen a massive increase in air transportation in the postwar years—and all-too-frequent accidents. The busy skies are likely to get busier into the twenty-first century.

Left: This photograph was taken on October 21, 1926, and shows the devastated coastline of Miami, following the great hurricane of 1926 which brought an abrupt halt to the Florida land boom. Hurricanes are a fact of life to those who live on the East Coast and the Gulf of Mexico. Throughout the season they build up over the ocean and race toward land and the fragile buildings that have been erected since the last hurricane.

Right: A fire at the Winecoff Hotel, Atlanta, Georgia, on December 9, 1946, when 116 people died. The hotel was thought to be fireproof, so no fire escapes were fitted. A family on the extreme top right can be seen climbing from the 15th to the 16th floor.

Right: Huge crowds gathered to view the wreck of the ill-fated luxury liner *Morro Castle* from the shores of Asbury Park, New Jersey. The massive ship mysteriously caught fire with the consequent loss of 134 lives.

The *Morro Castle*, run by the Ward Line, was a prime example of an accident waiting to happen. Due to the Depression, crew wages were low, all-round costs were slashed and corners were cut. Furthermore, Instead of having seventy-five percent American crewmen as required by law, the *Morro Castle* had far less.

On her last fateful cruise, for which her passengers had paid $65 each, she was in Cuba. But it was hurricane season, and one was heading her way, so on September 5, 1934, under the orders of her master, Captain Robert R. Willmott, she left Havana Harbor before schedule to avoid the hurricane. The master, although suffering from health problems, felt confident that he could outrun the storm. However, two evenings later he was found dead in his cabin and the First Mate William F. Warms took command of the vessel. In the early hours of the next morning, September 8, fire broke out in the Writing Room on the Promenade Deck. By this time the *Morro Castle* was about five miles off Sea Girt, New Jersey, but no SOS was sent out to call for help. Strong winds whipped the flames up and the inferno rapidly spread through the ship. The only lifeboats launched contained crew members; passengers were left to jump into the water. Some made it through the night in spite of the high seas and were pulled ashore by sightseers and volunteers when daylight came the next morning. The *Paramount*, a local fishing boat, managed to rescue more than sixty people. Other ships raced to the area to search for survivors.

The burning vessel was eventually taken under tow by the U.S. Coast Guard Cutter *Tampa* with the intention of taking her to the shelter of New York harbor. But by this time the hurricane had overtaken the rescue mission and the tow line snapped under the strain of the heavy seas. However, the *Morro Castle* could still float and she was taken by the currents to ground in front of Ashbury Park Convention Hall. The hull smoldered for weeks and was a great tourist attraction for thousands of curious onlookers. Criminal charges were brought against the Ward Line, the chief executive, and two crew members. They were found guilty and convicted but did not serve a prison sentence after a successful appeal. Meanwhile, 134 people had died horribly and unnecessarily.

Left: A couple sitting desolately among the wreck of their home at Highland Park, Rhode Island, after 100-mile-an-hour winds swept the Atlantic coast of North America in early October 1938.

Right: Windswept palm trees on a flooded beach as Hurricane Inez sweeps through Miami with winds of 100 mph. Inez was the most severe hurricane of the 1966 season.

Below: The aftermath of an explosion in Texas City in which 400 people were killed and more than 3,000 injured. A huge steel barge weighing 150 tons was propelled by the explosion from the ship basin to dry land, taking with it several cars. Photograph taken on April 19, 1947.

WOMEN

Historically, the lot of women in the United States has mirrored their lot in the industrialized world. Until the twentieth century, they held the role of homemaker and mother, running the home, producing and caring for their children and husbands, but were considered too frail for any more demanding role. It took the suffrage movement, two World Wars, and the postwar radical feminist movement to advance women to the station of equality with men they enjoy in law today.

Until the mid-19th century women in America had no legal status once they married, except through their husbands. A wife had no right to her own property or money, of which her husband took control; she could not sign a contract. Even as a single woman, an heiress was under the control of her father or brother. Her true role was in the home as wife and mother, a view wholly endorsed by the churches. Calls for womens' suffrage were loud in the second half of the nineteenth and early twentieth centuries, but Congress seemed indifferent to the cries. The situation was viewed differently out in the far West, where the importance of women in general was recognized and noted as a potent lure to get farming families to settle. In 1890, Wyoming became the first state in which women could vote (although Utah Territory had given them that right twenty years earlier). By 1914, ten Western states had given women the right to vote. Still nothing happened in the East, although it was proposed as a Constitutional amendment in 1878 and repeatedly thereafter. Before the 1916 election, both Republicans and Democrats said that women should have the right to vote, but they couldn't agree how to do this, so nothing was done.

The tide finally turned when American servicemen left to fight in Europe, and women had to leave their homes and take up jobs vacated by the soldiers. When the war was over and the men came back to their jobs, they were amazed at how well women had managed in their absence. Women had proven how hard and how well they could work, and it was this wartime effort that finally convinced sufficient people that women should have the right to vote.

This finally came with the Anthony Amendment, named after Susan B. Anthony, the campaigning abolitionist and temperance reformer. Modeled on the 15th Amendment, it gave women the right to vote and made sure that no individual state could rule otherwise and deny them this right. The Anthony Amendment became part of the Constitution in 1920.

Right: Group portrait of the 1955 Whittier College Homecoming Queen. She is wearing a tiara and cape and is surrounded by her court. All are wearing strapless evening gowns and hold bouquets.

Above: Members of the Women's Christian Temperance Union (WCTU) who marched on Washington D.C. to present a petition supporting prohibition, c. 1909. The WCTU was formed in 1874 primarily to stop the use of alcohol, but also campaigned on other issues such as the right of women to vote.

Right: A group of suffragettes enter the New York subway to catch the "penny tube" to Wall Street where they plan to make their protests in 1915. The state gave women the vote in 1917. Many of the women's suffrage groups disbanded after 1920 when they won the vote, allowing many other important issues—abortion rights, birth control, the right to sit on a jury—to fall by the wayside.

Far Right: A band of "news girls" of the Women's Suffrage Movement prepare to invade Wall Street armed with leaflets and slogans demanding votes for women in 1913. In 1848, Elizabeth Cady Stanton, together with Lucretia Mott, drew up and led the first women's rights convention in Seneca Falls, New York. There they called for laws giving women their rightful control over their own money and property, the right to divorce an unsuitable husband, the right to vote and educational and employment rights. Cady Stanton formed her own suffrage organization, which merged with that of Susan B. Anthony in 1890 to form the National American Women's Suffrage Association. Cady Stanton was also involved in marriage and divorce reform. She recognized that women needed a better position within marriage where they should be treated as equals. It took almost a hundred years for her views to achieve national acceptance.

Right: Harriet Beecher Stowe, the campaigning anti-slavery author of, among other books, *Uncle Tom's Cabin*, seen in 1865. She is surrounded by a group of like-minded anti-slavery workers.

Below: Society ladies ride bicycles around the fountain at City Hall while reenacting an old-style bicycle race in San Francisco in 1929. Several of the women are dressed as men, wearing suits and bowler hats, while the other women wear long dresses and wigs with bonnets attached.

Far Right: A Native American war worker, October 1918. In Native American society, a woman's role was to do the menial but essential tasks of homemaking and farming.

Above: Two women making pottery at Sparrow House in Plymouth, Pennsylvania.

Left: Mrs. Mary Bad Marriage of the Blackfeet tribe won a buckskin purse at the 1935 Glacier National Park Reservation Annual Agricultural and Industrial Fair for her bottled preparations.

Right: High society figure Slim Hawks (née Nancy Goss), former wife of director Howard Hawks, chatting with *Vogue* editor Diana Vreeland and her husband Reed, at Kitty Miller's New Year's Eve party in Park Avenue, New York, 1952.

Right: Ella Waldek jumps onto Nels Stewart's back and covers her eyes during a women's wrestling match. These two were among America's leading female wrestlers in February 1951.

Below: Florence Chadwick from San Diego, California, being given a rub-down before entering the water at St. Margaret's Bay, near Dover, Kent, for her attempt at a non-stop double crossing of the English Channel, October 11, 1955. She first swam both ways from France to England in 1950, and from England to France in 1951 and 1955.

Far Right: The University of Maryland football cheerleaders raising a shout for their team, c. 1950.

Above: Legendary rodeo star and sharpshooter Phoebe Mozee (1860–1926)—better known as "Annie Oakley." Photograph dated 1899. As a child in Ohio she learned to use a gun, and by the time she was a teenager Annie was giving sharpshooting exhibitions. She beat her famous rival Frank Butler in a shooting match but he could not have minded too much because they later married. Together they toured with a circus before joining Buffalo Bill's Wild West Show where she was one of the main attractions. They both retired with the Show's demise.

Left: Families enjoying the beach at Santa Monica, California, during summer 1890. The women wear full-length bathing costumes, including sun hats and stockings.

Inset: Cigar-smoking woman studying her hand while enjoying a game of cards in the sunshine on Coney Island, New York, in 1960.

Above: Two female welders at the Bethlehem-Fairfield Shipyards, Maryland, during World War II. Photograph dated May 1943.

Left: Nets for shallow-water fishermen being made by their wives and daughters in the early 1950s. The finished nets are better, the original caption states, as well as much cheaper, than shop-bought ones. Their husbands fish the brackish flats between Portsmouth Island and the mainland of North Carolina.

Right: A health worker for the U.S. Food and Drug Administration checks on a sample in a laboratory to ensure that it is safe for human consumption; a 1945 photograph.

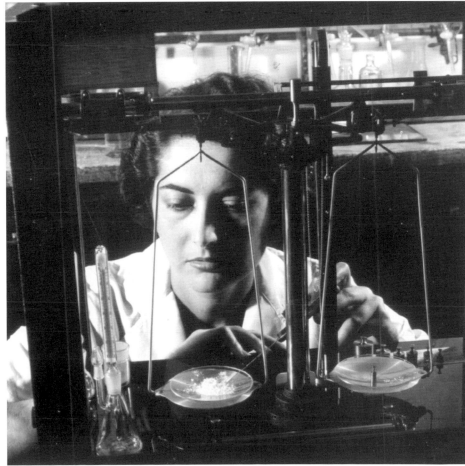

CHILDREN

Children are the future and hope of every country, but in the past children in America have not always enjoyed an easy life. The lot of many poor immigrant children was a life—and all too often death—of hardship and labor in the mines and sweatshops of their new country. Children, alongside their mothers and big sisters, were put to work in mines and factories—particularly in the cotton industry—across the country. The great attraction for employers was the cheapness of their labor, especially of immigrant slum children whose parents could not afford to be fussy about their working conditions.

Many people were deeply concerned about the abuse of child labor but were unable—except in exceptional local circumstances—to do anything about it. Some of the earliest legislation concerning children was passed in 1847 in New Hampshire, Pennsylvania, and Massachusetts, which forbade the employment of children for more than ten hours a day without their parents' consent, but this was only a token gesture and not followed up by any other states.

In 1900 there were 1.7 million children under the age of sixteen in employment; this had gone up to two million under the age of fifteen by 1911. In that year there were over 15,000 boys under the age of sixteen working long hours in the coal mines. Many action committees were formed, especially linked to the womens' movement, for whom child protection was a natural companion. At last, in 1904, the National Child Labor Committee was formed to campaign specifically for child welfare, particularly in respect of employment, and to coordinate the many different child welfare groups working in isolation from each other around the country. Their success was such that within ten years, twenty-five states had legislated a range of restrictions on the exploitation of children in the workplace.

The first federal child labor law was championed by President Woodrow Wilson as part of his package of improving working conditions in America. Known as the Keating-Owen Act, it was passed by Congress in August 1916. It banned the employment of children under fourteen working in businesses engaged in interstate commerce. The businessmen who employed the child labor were outraged at this restriction to their right to employ whoever they wanted, and lobbied hard to get the ban overturned as unconstitutional by the Supreme Court in 1918, in spite of the opposition of Congress. The Second Child Labor Act of 1919 suffered the same fate in 1922.

Right: Two boys pulling and pushing wagons loaded with scrap wood on a city street in 1910.

Right: Alaskan boys standing in front of "Adam House," under which many people believe lie the last remains of the Aleut's legendary tree of life.

Left: An elderly woman of a Native American tribe, with a young child in 1910.

Below: A young boy from the Columbus boys' choir school takes his lunch and reads on a bus in the 1950s.

Franklin Roosevelt turned his attention to the problem of child labor in the course of his reforms in 1933. When drawing up codes for the cotton industry, he forbade the use of child labor in the mills. Similarly, when he looked at the coal industry, child labor was banished from the mines. Children had been particularly useful in workplaces such as mines where they could squeeze into shafts where no adult could fit to grub out the spoil.

Today, child labor is still a world issue. Insatiable consumer demand in the United States and the developed world requires commodities produced at market prices, and to sell these commodities at prices and still make a profit, companies search for cheap labor in the developing world—and that often means children. Large multinationals are often identified as the major culprits, and the revulsion that child labor engenders means the issue is unlikely to go away quietly in the twenty-first century.

Education has been an important factor in American politics and has always been highly valued by Americans. Reformers were quick to advocate education as a means to Americanize young immigrants and assimilate them into society. This was especially crucial when the immigrant families were from non-English-speaking countries. In part to remedy this, and to keep children off the streets and out of the sweat shops, compulsory school attendance laws were passed. Consequently, by 1880 almost seventy-five percent of school-age children were attending school—although children belonging to an ethnic minority, such as African-Americans, Native Americans, and Asians, were placed in segregated schools. By 1896 this was put into law, and it would take until the second half of the twentieth century and the civil rights movement for education to be desegregated.

Right: A young resident at the Tascosa boys' ranch in Texas learns to read under the watchful eye of a teacher. The ranch was set up as an alternative to reform school, to provide a refuge for boys from broken homes who might otherwise turn to a life of crime. Photograph dated February 1951.

Below: Three little Amish boys take it in turns to have a go on the "Champion" ride outside a grocery store in 1955.

Far Right: A teenager takes a hearty drink of milk from the family fridge in 1956.

Above: New York children splash about in a flooded street after the police opened the fire hydrants to beat the unbearable heat of summer, August 2, 1961.

Left and Right: Ten years later, New York children cool off and have fun in the same way in New York City's East Harlem, October 27, 1971. Some things never change.

PART 6

AMERICA AT WORK

OFFICE

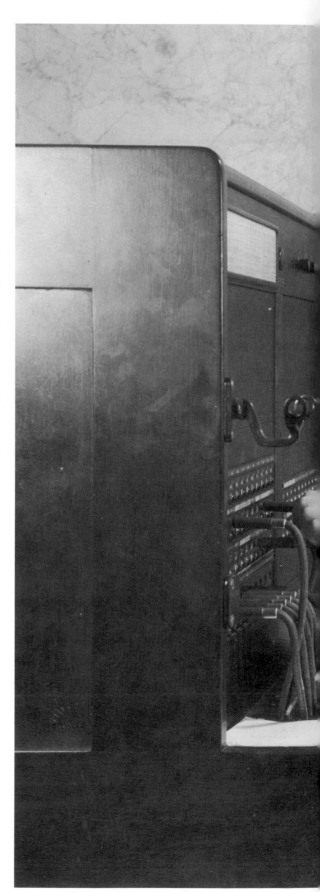

In the nineteenth century office work was "white collar" work because it required an ability to read and write at a time when not everyone did, coupled with the fact that the job was indoors and involved no manual labor. Another important difference was that such workers were usually salaried rather than paid in cash at the end of each day, and sometimes were even professionally qualified. Consequently, at a time when eighty percent of men and forty percent of women could only write their names but not much else, office work had a cachet and status. Offices were also the first places that women were accepted as workers in their own right, and one of the first professional places (outside teaching) where women could hold authority over men. Moreover, the work involved was acceptable to protective fathers and husbands, as the women were kept away from the public eye and not subjected to physical work. Women themselves appreciated it as an escape from the routine of housework that allowed them a degree of financial independence.

Much early office work involved routine bookkeeping, and it was not until the invention of the typewriter that clerical work really exploded. The typewriter was devised by Christopher Sholes, a Milwaukee printer, and two friends, Carlos Glidden and Samuel W. Soule, in 1867. They patented the invention but sold the rights to a pair of entrepreneurs, Densmore and Yost, who took the idea to the Remington Gun Company, already successful manufacturers of guns and sewing machines. The first commercially successful typewriter was called the "Sholes and Gliden Type-Writer," but the early model was difficult to use and was no quicker than writing by hand; it also only wrote in capitals. The typewriter was offered at $125 each, and in the first five years of production, only 5,000 machines were sold. However, the Remington company improved the machine and within ten years the typewriter had become an essential piece of office equipment. It was not displaced until the wholesale uptake of the personal computer well over a hundred years later.

Previous Page: Workmen loading fish at New York's Fulton Fish Market, c. 1950.

Right: A smiling switchboard operator cheerfully connects a call on her switchboard, c. 1940. Jobs working on the switchboard were sought after and even had a touch of glamor about them. Employers looked for a good telephone manner and a cheerful and clear speaking voice. Discretion was an important factor as well, because the operator could listen in on other people's conversations.

Right: A female telephone operator sits at a long switchboard; she is wearing a headset, pearl necklace and high heels, c. 1922.

Below: A tea tester samples tea, 1904.

Bottom: The traditional view of office work— a typist. In fact, this is a telegraph operator sitting at a desk typing a telegram, c. 1920.

Other inventions which revolutionized office work include the adding machine, devised by William S. Burroughs in 1891. This immediately saved hours of counting and calculating by clerks and enabled bookeeping to be kept by less-skilled mathematicians than previously possible. The cash register was invented by James S. Ritty in Ohio in 1879. This, too, completely changed the face of retailing, although out in the shop floor where the public could marvel at it, rather than behind the scenes.

Today, when so many people work in offices, the cachet of being a "white" collar worker has been reduced somewhat!

BH
BUSH TERMINAL

"LT"
NATIONAL LEAD
COM.

GGN A
GENERAL CABLE CORP

D
PUBLICATIONS

1 0 1

9 2 ¾

1 5 ⅞

"SCD"
STANDARD OIL CALIF.

HSY
HERSHEY CHOCOLATE CORP

5 3 ⅜

4 7 ⅜

PRESENTED BY
W. H. DO

Left: A broker at the Wall Street Stock Exchange indicates her buying and selling prices, c. 1929. Professional women often found it hard to be accepted in a man's world, but with increasing access to higher education, the doors of the institutions could not stay shut to them forever. In the nineteenth century, unable to get into colleges and medical schools, many women-only colleges were established with the specific aim of giving girls as good an education as their male counterparts. Interestingly, the great women's colleges were founded on fortunes made in industry and commerce, unlike the men's, which were religious establishments. Vassar was founded in 1861, Smith in 1870, Wellesley in 1870, and Bryn Mawr in 1885. Today, many girls outperform boys from the earliest school ages.

Right: An American nurse in the Red Cross summer uniform, 1917. At this period it was still unusual to find women qualified as doctors and the only medical service they were allowed to provide was that of nursing.

Below: The entrance to 40 Wall Street, c. 1950.

Left: A snack bar serving food and drinks opposite the First National City Bank on New York's Wall Street, June 1964.

Right: A broker at work on the floor of the Stock Exchange on Wall Street, New York, June 1964.

Below: A businessman working at an IBM office computer with two components: at left, an accounting machine, and at right, a reproducing summary punch, c. 1965. Today, most office workers have seen mainframe computers swapped for networked PCs, and the future of the office is in doubt. Why pay for an employee's light, heat, and desk when they can work from the comfort of their own home without the commuting?

INDUSTRY

The industrial revolution reached the United States in 1790, when Samuel Slater built a cotton mill at Pawtucket, Rhode Island. Initially based on their European counterparts, the early part of the nineteenth century saw American business ideas and production increase. The advent of the railways played its part, but industry in America was given its greatest impetus by the Civil War. While it brought misery to many, businessmen were able to profit from the trade in munitions, and wartime contractors laid the basis for their fortunes in this period. With these profits came the capital to start new businesses.

These burgeoning industries were protected. High-tariff trade barriers were erected to protect them from external competition. These lasted in various forms from the late 1860s to the 1930s. Furthermore, government was effectively barred from interfering in corporate civil rights by the 14th Amendment to the Constitution. Government was not allowed to "impair contract," which meant that it could not set standards of pay or working conditions for employees. Government attempts, therefore, to regulate employment were unsuccessful even when tried through the courts. All this meant was that workers had few civil rights and could be exploited more or less at will by their employers, who in turn were able to become wealthy on the profits. Working conditions generally were appalling, and workplace accidents frequent and often fatal. Campaigners lobbied for better working conditions to little avail—employers always seemed to have the funds to buy more stocks but never enough to improve the lives of those on whose backs the profits were made. Corruption was widespread and endemic in big business.

By the turn of the century the United States had the largest economy and was the richest country in the world. The booming industrial economy of the early twentieth century led to the widespread development of manufacturing industry. The new "sciences" of advertising and marketing were developed at this time. Employers started to look seriously at how to rationalize the working process to its best effect, and how to manage the workers and staff both on the factory floor and in business offices. The latest technology was embraced to develop factory manufacturing lines to make products as economically as possible, and then to warehouse and

Right: Women rivet heaters and passers on ship construction work in the Navy Yard at Puget Sound, Seattle, Washington, May 29, 1919. As men were called up to fight in Europe during World War I, women moved in to many previously male-dominated industries to keep the factory lines moving and provide essential equipment.

Right: Child employees standing in rows in front of a brick mill building in Georgia, c. 1910. Even the meager wages that children could bring into a household could make all the difference between the family eating or going hungry.

Below Right: A diver being lowered onto a wreck, c. 1900.

Far Right: Auto workers lowering the body of a Model T onto its chassis on an assembly line ramp outdoors at the Ford Motor Company, Highland Park, Michigan, c. 1914.

Following Page: Mina Van Winkle, the head of the Lecture Bureau of Food Administration in California, c. 1918.

distribute the goods so as to get to the consumer as quickly and cheaply as possible. Competition was the spur.

Large corporations started to develop and were so successful in the American market that they started to export abroad and earn foreign currency—all boosting the American economy. The middle class started to expand and for the first time they had sufficient disposable income to spend on consumer goods—previously the domain only of the rich.

Before the turn of the century, most companies had been relatively small, family-owned concerns, but in the new economy, the money men started to move in and buy up entire companies and merge them into others—corporations were born and run by financiers. Speculation on the stock market fueled the boom and times were good. Such mergers and takeovers quickly produced huge corporations and monopolies and giant trusts, as well as businessmen such as Rockefeller in oil and Carnegie in steel. Their personal financial power gave them extraordinary political clout. The railroads, public utilities, and mineral industries became characterized by a few giant companies. A new type of company, the holding company, was devised. In this way one particular company owned sufficient stock in a number of other companies so as to be able to control their operations. By 1904 there were seven massive American holding companies, the biggest being the first billion-dollar company, United States Steel; the others were American Sugar Refining, Amalgamated Copper, American Smelting and Refining, Consolidated Tobacco, Standard Oil, and International Mercantile and Marine.

The 1920s were good times for the rich, but there was too much money circulating around the economy. Factories and farms were overproducing. Speculation was rife. High tariffs prevented foreign imports from making much impression on the country. The economy overheated and collapsed dramatically for many people in October 1929. The Great Depression started and lasted ten long, grim years. President Franklin D. Roosevelt's New Deal slowly brought about improvements, but the economy would not pick up again until World War II.

The war led to jobs in the armament, aircraft, and automobile industries, as well as in steel and coal. The postwar boom saw dramatic improvements to standards of living across the length and breadth of America. By the time the boom finished, American lifestyle had reached a level previously unattained by ordinary people all over the the world. The late twentieth century would see many heavy industries lose their viability—particularly mining, shipbuilding, and steel manufacturing—but to offset this came the increase in leisure industries. It remains to be seen whether the twenty-first century will continue the boom and bust cycle of its predecessor.

It's a great thing to be a club girl,
And to know all they know—
It's a great thing to be a club girl,
And to watch the young plants grow;
For we'll make the best better
And work with head, heart, hand.
It's a great, great thing to be a club girl,
Health and wealth we'll command.

We planted our tenth of an acre
And tended it many hot days.
But now as we bring in the harvest
We're glad that we worked for it pays.
Cho. Canning, canning, come see our 4H Brand, just see
Canning, canning, the girls canning club are we.

Left: A woman folding U.S. Army blankets, c. 1945. After the war many employers kept women on because they found they could pay them less than the men.

Far Left: A female car worker cleans out a grinding machine in a Pennsylvania metal shop during World War II. Before the war, women were not employed in heavy industry. Large numbers of women took on jobs for the first time during World War II, but the numbers of single women were insufficient for the amount of work. Consequently, the government actually encouraged married women to work in the public sectors. To help them do so, child care centers were opened to look after children while their mothers were at work. During the war years (1941–45) about six and a half million women—many of them housewives—took jobs for the first time. By war's end, women comprised fifty-seven percent of employees.

Below: Two women polishing heat-treated aluminum pistons before they are submitted to a hardness test for airplane engines, c. 1950.

Above: The cutthroat competition for passengers meant that airlines used every means possible to attract customers. In the front line were the stewardesses. Southwest Airlines of Texas stipulated that their stewardesses must wear hot pants and leather boots or they wouldn't get the job. The airline's motto was "sex sells seats." Even the drinks they served were given racy names such as "Passion Punch" and "Love Potion." The feminist movement was outraged at such sexist ploys and the airlines eventually had to stop such brazen techniques to attract customers.

Right: A mass-production line at the newly opened Electronics Communications Inc. plant at St. Petersburg, Florida. Several hundred workers were employed on government contracts when this photograph was taken on April 25, 1966.

LABOR

America experienced a huge building boom in the mid-nineteenth century, as towns and cities swelled to accommodate thousands of immigrants and new settlers. This provided a vast potential market for unskilled labor, but in the 1850s many Americans—both old and new—wanted to benefit from the new lands being opened up in the West. So many people migrated that a real labor shortage existed until the first waves of mass immigration to the United States took up the vacant unskilled jobs.

Between 1840 and 1870, two million Irish, escaping the potato famines at home, arrived in America, virtually all of whom were looking for work. Unskilled jobs, although not well paid, gave the workers the opportunity to establish themselves and their families in relative security with an improved standard of living. Organized labor was ultimately responsible for seeing that wages for the unskilled workers rose steadily between 1860 and 1890. They would slump in the 1890s, then rise again between 1897 and 1914 at the start of World War I. Collective labor was able to reduce the working week from approximately sixty-six hours in 1860 to fifty-five hours in 1914. Not everyone benefited. Skilled labor usually found jobs easier to come by and better paid; those belonging to a union benefited from better working conditions as well, and workers in the North were considerably better off than those in the South.

Despite the reluctance of male society to allow women to work outside the home, women comprised the majority of workers in the textile mills of New England even before the Civil War. They worked in a wide variety of jobs and earned only a quarter of what a man earned—hence the mill owners' willingness to employ women workers. It was because women were subjected to poorer working conditions and lower pay that they were among the first workers to agitate for better conditions and they were often strike leaders and organizers of labor unions.

As in all industrialized nations, the course of labor politics through the last half of the nineteenth and the early twentieth centuries was not straightforward. The fight for better working conditions created unions which sometimes grew megalithic and often corrupt; the battles between bosses and unions did not often improve the lot of the worker, but certainly gave the union leaders political clout.

What is in no doubt is that the United States was the powerhouse of the world during this period, rising to be the greatest industrial

Right: A young worker manufacturing parts using a machine tool, c. 1940.

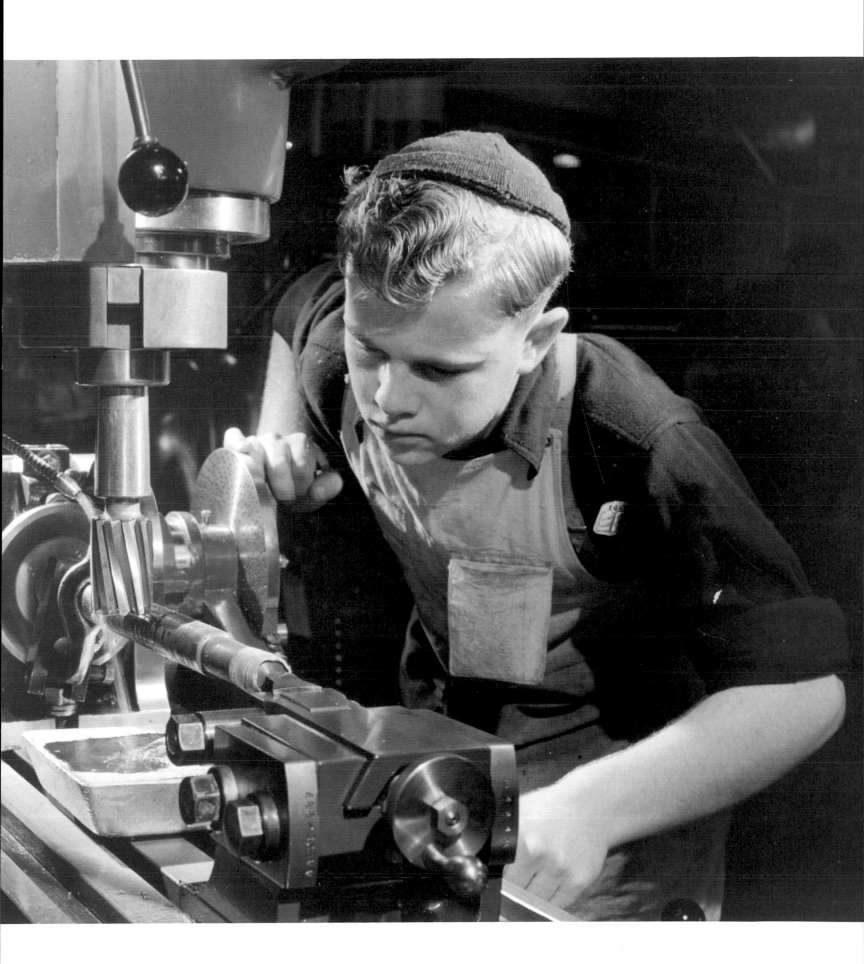

power on earth. Fueled by the benefits of two world wars, both of which were won through quantity of production rather than quality of equipment, the United States was able to survive the "bust" years of capitalism, and enjoy the substantial "booms"—particularly during the time after World War II when consumerism triumphed.

Today many of the heavy industries—steel, shipbuilding, and mining—have dwindled, but new technologies have funded continuing good times. Computers may have affected the labor force through use of robots and computer-assisted design, but they have also created a world where leisure time has generated a massive new range of industries, from theme parks to shopping malls. The latest industries—those spawned by the Internet—may have been brought back down to earth for the time being, and the number of people who have lost a million dollars, on paper at least in the form of stock options, increased a hundredfold, but this retrenchment will be shortlived. There are fewer physcial jobs in the modern labor world as machinery has taken much of the sheer muscle-work out of the jobs market, but there will always be a demand for good workers as the brain of computers can never replace human brawn.

Above: A child worker in a textile factory, 1910.

Left: A group of women sewing the wings for an early Boeing aircraft in a plant in Seattle, Washington, 1918. They can hardly have realized that they were working for a company that would become the "Planemaker to the World." Today, Boeing is based in Chicago and builds the most popular civil aircraft of all time.

Right: Dr. Stephen S. Wise, the Rabbi of the Free Synagogue, working with his son as a laborer in the shipyard of the Luder Marine Construction Company in Stamford, Connecticut, during World War I, July 1918.

Left: A Pennsylvania Railroad engineer leans out of the window of his cab in 1924. The railroads provided thousands of Americans with employment, not just in building and running them, but also in mining and manufacturing. The ever-increasing demand for coal and iron—and then, as technology changed, steel—created new industries and new jobs. Towns grew up around the mines and manufacturing centers and soon entire areas depended on the railroad for jobs. When the railroad industry began to contract, hit by cheap gas and competitive air transport, many of these industries died.

Above: A shirtless worker grips a hoisting ball while working on the construction of the the Empire State Building's mooring mast.

Right: A striking zinc miner in Columbus County, Kansas, carrying a protest poster, May 1936.

Far Right: A line of men inside the state employment service office in San Francisco, California, January 1938.

Top: A day laborer resting on a sign near a railroad platform in Raymondville, Texas, February 1939.

Above: An Ohio woman works as a Baltimore and Ohio Railroad mechanic's assistant on a train during World War II, c. 1943.

Right: Two porters or "redcaps" pause to chat during their shift at the Pennsylvania Railroad Station, 1942.

Above: These men are hoping for a chance to do some manual work. Nearby, a couple of derelicts lie prone, c. 1950.

Left: A lumberjack at work near Effie, Minnesota, September 1937.

Right: Engineers at work positioning a drill in the lowermost gallery of the Grand Coulee Dam, Washington State, c. 1955.

Far Left: One of the last mountain mailmen using a mule to deliver the mail to a log cabin on the edge of Kentucky, c. 1940.

Left: The "Silver Floor" at Tiffany's in New York, one of the most famous jewelry stores in the world, c. 1955.

Below: A window cleaner at work on the RCA Building, Rockefeller Center, in New York City, May 2, 1961.

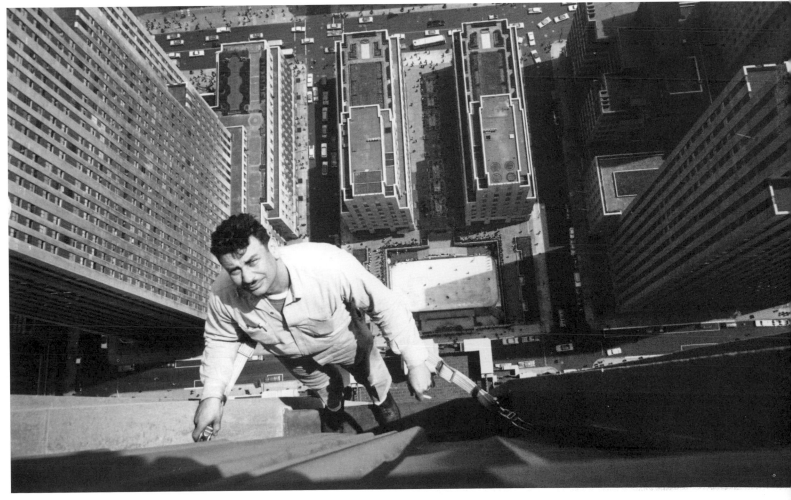

FARMING

Across most of America during the nineteenth century, times were good for the small family farmers; most made a comfortable living and enjoyed a physically hard but rewarding life. Following the Civil War, this situation differed for farmers in the South. Many small holders there were forced into debt-slavery which made farming a hard, if not impossible, living. When the price of cotton plummeted, the debts got greater and the farmers' dissatisfaction with the government intensified; poverty and disease were the norm in many homes. Education, which had been seen as a way out of poverty even in rural communities, had led to an increase in schooling and education, but even this hope of escape fell by the wayside as grim reality sank in.

Conditions across the United States started to change after the 1880s. Farmers, especially those working in the West, felt aggrieved by the increasingly heavy debts with which they were saddled. The cost of using the railroad for getting their produce to market was high, and even when transportation prices fell it was typically the middlemen who reaped the benefit, not the farmers. The high cost of transportation was a major farming grievance; furthermore, it seemed that everyone was getting rich on agriculture except the farmers. The bankers, railroads, middlemen, merchants, suppliers, processors and shippers, all coupled with the increasing drought, roused the farmers into forming the Farmers' Alliance. Starting in Texas, the Alliance for the first time lobbied collectively in Congress, organized co-operative purchasing and marketing and provided advice on better husbandry and technological innovations, particularly on advances and use of farm machinery, as well as providing a social focus for the farming community. For the first time, farmers had a voice that demanded attention.

After the 1880s, people started to drift away from the land as drought and mechanization reduced the need for agricultural workers. For those who chose to stay rather than abandon the country for an

Right: A farmer using a cultivator in his carrot patch, c. 1955

Left: Farming has always been hot, physical work; here a farmer takes a break to wipe the sweat from his brow, c. 1930.

Top: In open country, a farming family stands on a combine harvester while horses forage in the stubble, 1900. At harvest, everyone had to help to bring in the crop.

Above: The Newton Square Unit of the Women's Land Army in Pennsylvania, 1918.

urban, industrial existence, life was still hard but could be rewarding—Americans have always prided themselves on their self-sufficiency and self-reliance and the small farmer exemplified these virtues. When times were hard economically, such as during the long years of the Depression, farmers and their families were usually able to survive better than townspeople because they could at least grow their own food and survive off the land, albeit from hand to mouth.

Above: A farmer at work in his corn field in Indiana, April 1938.

Left: Cotton pickers at work on Delta and Pine Land in Bolivar County, Mississippi, c. 1938.

Right: An elderly farm worker sieving grain, c. 1940.

Following Page: A group of cattlemen at an auction of prize beef steers and breeding stock at the San Angelo fat stock show in San Angelo, Texas, March 1940.

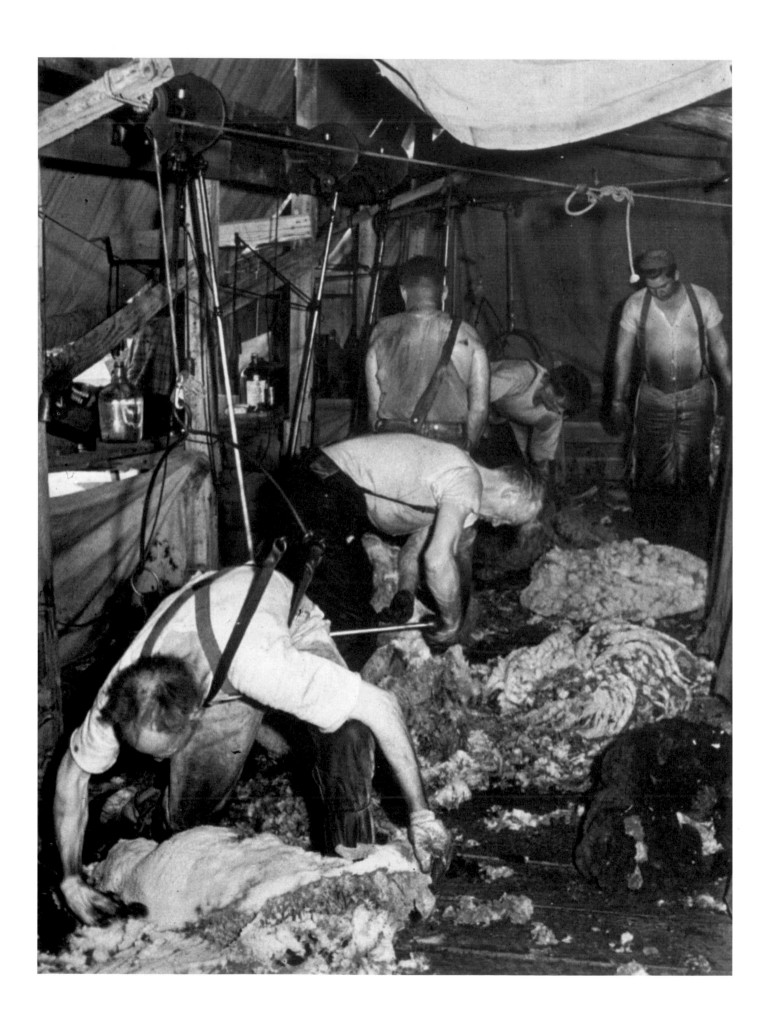

Left: Sheep shearers at work on a ranch in Malheur County, Oregon, May 1941.

Right: A woman picking cotton by the Mississippi near Memphis, 1950.

Below: A typical harvest scene of bales of straw and sacks of grain, c. 1950.

Right: Berry pickers from Philadelphia sitting in the back of their labor contractor's truck in Burlington County, New Jersey, c. 1955.

Far Right: Reverend Hoy worked as a farm hand in return for supplies when he first arrived in the area; now he owns his own ten-acre farm in central Ohio, c. 1955.

Below: A Hopi woman watches over a herd of sheep and goats by a sand dune in the Arizona desert, c. 1955.

TECHNOLOGY

The economic revolution was fueled in part by new inventions and technological discoveries following the new era introduced by the Industrial Revolution. Brilliant and inquisitive minds made breakthroughs in all manner of technologies and the world became a very different place within a few years thanks to new travel technologies, the understanding and control of electricity, and production line assembly, among many other developments.

Due to the drive, individualism, and entrepreneurship of Americans, industry in the United States was not bound by ancient practices and was instead uniquely adaptable and amenable to new ideas and changes in technology. Moreover, American businessmen were ready, willing, and able to make the most of the latest ideas regardless of whether they came from Europe or America. One significant indication of this is that in the 1890s an astonishing annual average of 21,000 patents were taken out by American inventors. Furthermore, undergraduates were pouring out of the universities and into industry; in 1870 there were 52,300 graduates, by 1900 this figure had risen to 237,600.

The great leap forward in technology was accelerated by the harnessing of electricity. Electricity had been discovered as early as 1807 by Sir Humphrey Davy, but in common with so many scientific advances, nobody knew how to apply a practical use to it. That was until Thomas Edison applied his unique mind to the problem. He established a laboratory at Menlo Park, New Jersey in 1876 with the specific objective of using teams of researchers to discover new products which could be sold to an eagerly awaiting public. The laboratory was a great success and was responsible for many inventions, including the storage battery, the phonoscope, the electric locomotive, the motion picture projector, and perhaps most important of all, the carbon filament lamp. Edison then developed the electrical circuit with individual power switches for different outlets and within six years over two million electric lightbulbs were illuminating America. In the early days electricity could only be transmitted for a mile or two from the generator; then George M. Westinghouse developed the technology of alternating current and transformers so that high voltage electric current could be transferred quickly and cheaply across the country (1886). Other

Right: Two banks of high power water-cooled amplifying tubes, part of the high power portion of a radio telephone transmitter. This apparatus was used in the transatlantic telephone tests by the American Telephone and Telegraph Company and the Radio Corporation of America. March 19, 1926.

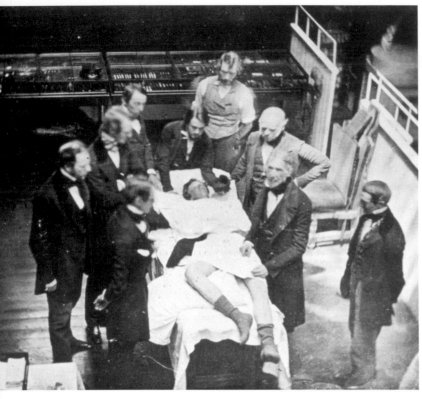

inventions improving the electrical technology followed quickly: the electric motor created power (1888), dynamos were improved and electricity was developed in such a way as to be used by electric streetcars (1887), electric elevators (1889) enabled skyscrapers to become practical.

These and many other technological developments allowed the American economy to explode in the twentieth century. This was helped by the lack of internal trade restrictions, so large scale production and cross-country distribution costs could be slashed. An entire new business philosophy developed to make the most of these advantages, companies grew into large, efficiently managed corporations which used the latest production methods and advanced technology, as well as rationalization of the production process to produce cheap products. For the first time truly competitive marketing and advertising enticed the public into buying products that they did not necessarily need.

America became the first real consumer society, more than rich enough to export the excess abroad to an ever-willing world. The only losers in all this were the workers themselves who endured often harsh employment and living conditions in the cause of economic success.

Top: Dr. John Collins Warren (second from the left) treating a surgery patient under ether, which was pioneered at the hospital in 1846. Behind him is the physician and poet Oliver Wendell Holmes (1809–1894), the father of the Supreme Court of Justice. Massachusetts General Hospital, c. 1847.

Right: American scientist George Washington Carver (1864–1943), the son of a slave from Missouri, working at the Tuskegee Facility in Alabama, 1896.

Far Right: Thomas Edison on the left, inventor and physicist. He personally took out over 1,000 patents for inventions ranging from the gramaphone to incandescant light bulbs. Here he is looking at the first phonograph, which he invented sixty years earlier. With him is Governor Moore of New Jersey. August, 1927.

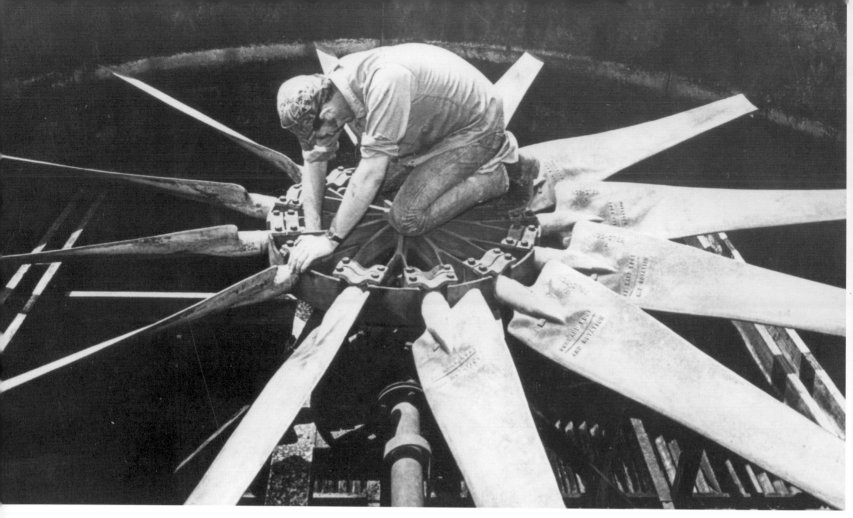

Above: An engineer at work on a 16-foot fan, which was used to remove natural gases from 17 huge engines at the Tenneco Gas Pipeline Company's plant at East Bernard, Texas.

Right: Smiling messengers sitting on their new motor scooters outside a Western Union telegraph office, c. 1940.

Far Right: The mass production of Bell Airacobra ground attack fighter aircraft, at the new Bell Aircraft's Niagara Falls assembly plant, c. 1941.

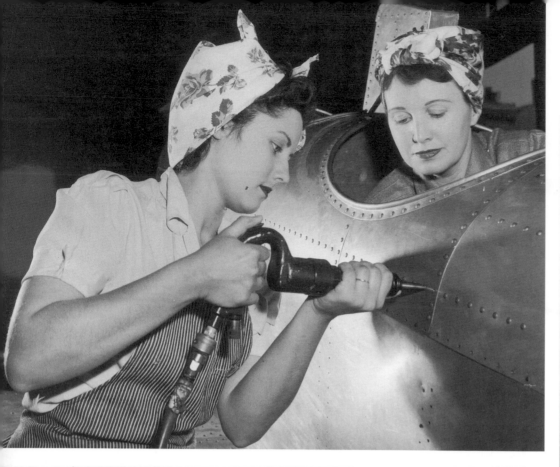

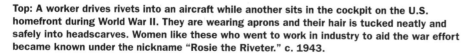

Top: A worker drives rivets into an aircraft while another sits in the cockpit on the U.S. homefront during World War II. They are wearing aprons and their hair is tucked neatly and safely into headscarves. Women like these who went to work in industry to aid the war effort became known under the nickname "Rosie the Riveter." c. 1943.

Above: Three members of Women Flyers of America Inc., look on while their instructor explains the fundamentals. The organization had been asked by the U.S. Army to submit names of women with more than 200 flying hours who may be capable of ferrying planes.

Right: Female factory workers stand on wooden platforms as they rivet the outer shell of a bomb-bay section at Chrysler Corporation's DeSoto Bomber Plant, June 11, 1942.

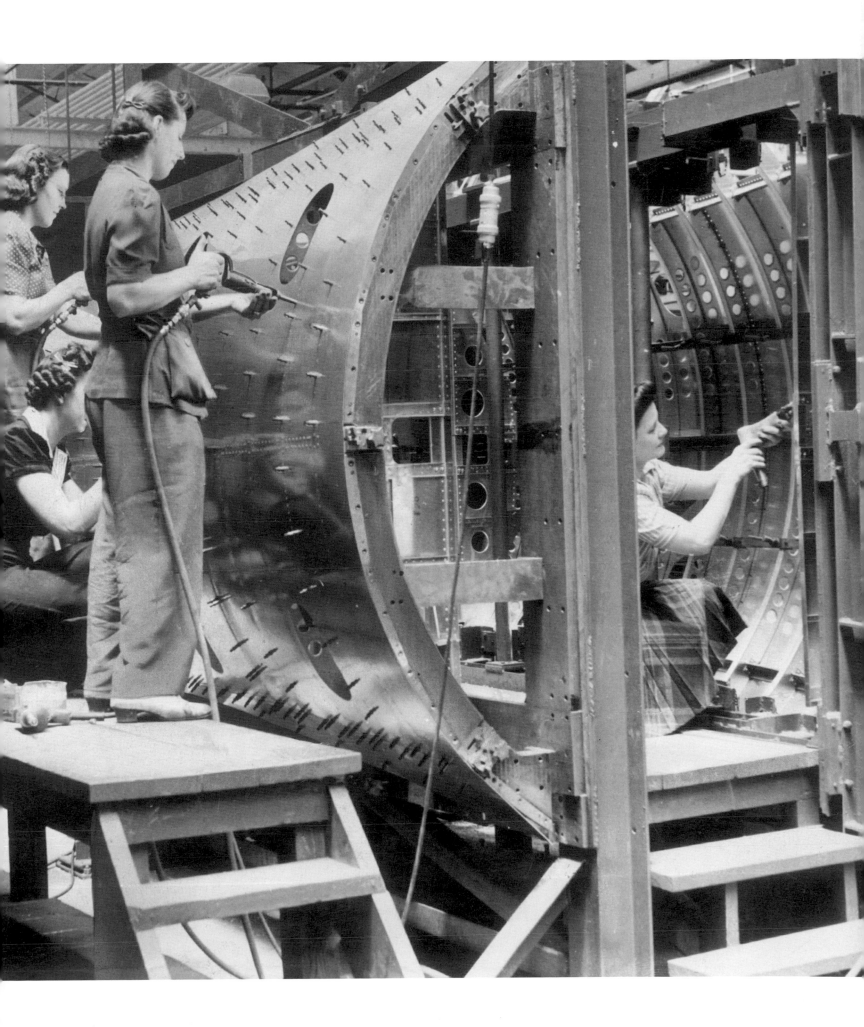

Top: Radiochemist at the Argonne National Laboratory working with radioactive materials, 1950.

Right: Anthropomorphs, man-made men being assembled by American aviation experts. With rubber skins, they are of human size, weight, and shape, with electronic equipment in their chests and stomach cavities to record information of use to pilots during high-speed ejection. April 9, 1958.

Far Right: Inventor Sterling Newberry displays his "fly's eye" lens at the General Electric Research Center at Schenectady, New York. The device is a compound electron lens 2 inches in diameter and half an inch thick, composed of 1,024 smaller lenses, like a fly's eye (which contains 4,000 small lenses). Each of the small lenses focuses a separate electronic image on a fine grain film, allowing enormous information storage potential in a very small space. April 17, 1969.

COWBOYS

The great plains of America where the buffalo once roamed were a gift for cattle farmers. The herds could graze unhindered for as far as the eye could see, and beyond. After the Native Americans were forcibly expelled from their traditional lands, huge areas were open for exploitation by cattle farmers and their work hands, the cowboys. The Great Plains in particular proved invaluable—vast rolling cattle country full of rich buffalo grass ideal for fattening cattle. Soon after the release of the lands, immense herds of longhorns grazed the grounds and rapidly spread in numbers.

The cowboys lived alongside the cattle out in the wild country, only going into town on the weekends—dressed in their best clothes—to drink, gamble, and consort with women. The cowboys herded and tended the cattle with techniques of roping, branding, and herding learned, in large part, from Mexican cattle workers who had done such work for generations.

Following the peace after the Civil War, Chicago became the chief destination for cattle; there they would be sold at high prices to the slaughterhouses. In 1866, a trail known as the Long Drive was launched, to great success. The cattle were driven from all over the Great Plains, anything up to 1,500 miles from Texas to the railhead in western Missouri. All along the trail, cattle towns sprung up to cater to the new trade, the most famous of which was Dodge City.

The Chisholm and Western Trails were the main cattle routes. But these trails took the cattle through Kansas and over lands belonging to farmers hostile to Texas cattlemen, and confrontations could be bloody. Then, as the railroads were extended further into America, the long cattle drives became shorter.

Soon, cattle were being grazed on the ranges of Wyoming, Colorado, Dakota Territory, Nebraska, and Montana, as well as in Texas and Kansas. But the good times could not last; over-grazing became a serious problem and cattle were pushed further and further afield in an attempt to find fresh pasture lands. The cowboys also found a new enemy in sheep, which grazed on the same lands as the cattle. After the invention of barbed wire in 1874, enclosing land to contain the sheep and keep out the cattle became cheap and easy, and within six years much of the Plains were enclosed and the heyday of the cowboy was over. The final straw for the cattlemen came in the winters of 1885-6 and 1886-7, which were so cold that cattle froze and starved to death by the thousands.

Right: Cowboys watering their horses on the Turkey Track Ranch in Texas, 1910.

Above: African-American cowpunchers outside Bonham, Texas, 1885.

Right: A Native American cowboy in Montana, c. 1850.

Far Right, Above: A Texas cowboy resting on his horse in the Bar Diamond Ranch, 1905.

Far Right, Below: Cowboys at work at the Matador Ranch, Texas, 1908.

Above: Cowboys drinking in a bar in Alpine, Texas, May 1939.

Left: Scottish-born Reverend McNab Wilson was adopted into the Blackfoot tribe during a ceremony at Chief Two Guns's White Calf Lodge, Glacier Park Reservation, Montana. The reverend worked in a gambling house before becoming a preacher under the Presbyterian Board of Home Missions and traveled the reservation on his painted pony. March 16, 1932.

Right: A calf branded during a round-up at the Brewster Arnold Ranch, near Birney, Montana, June 1939.

SPORTS

One of America's greatest passions is with sports and athletes. The United States, through its college sports scholarships and the importance of sports in its educational curriculum, has achieved excellence in most areas of sporting endeavor, and population changes—the immigration of so many Mexicans and Central Americans—may bring success in those world sports such as men's soccer, until now struggling to maintain a U.S. presence at the highest level.

The three quintessential American games are baseball, basketball, and football. All were invented in the United States and all are dominated by American-born players; each sport's "world championship" is limited to the involvement of North American teams. These three sports define the year for American sports fans.

Baseball, it is generally accepted, was devised in 1839 by West Point cadet Abner Doubleday, who drew up the first diamond at Cooperstown, New York. Today it is played all over the world, and not just by expatriates or U.S. military forces serving overseas, although both have helped popularize the sport.

Gridiron football started in the mass ball games of the eighteenth century brought to America by European settlers. Thse were played with rough and ready enthusiasm and often became violent. These games gradually became more formalized until football emerged as a winter college sport in the mid-nineteenth century. The first rules were drawn up at Princeton College in 1867 for a game against Rutgers University.

Basketball was invented by Canadian James A. Naismith in 1891. A physical training instructor at the YMCA in Springfield, Massachusetts, he was concerned about the students' lack of physical fitness and exercise during the long, cold winter months, so he devised a game to counteract the problem. He simply nailed a peach basket onto the balcony at either end of the gymnasium, drew up some simple rules, and basketball has never looked back.

Previous Page: Shuffleboard in the sunshine at a resort in Miami Beach, Florida, c. 1940. Shuffleboard was introduced about 1913 at Daytona Beach, Florida, as a game on land; previously it had been played on board ships as a deck entertainment. So popular was the game that it spread rapidly through the United States, particularly in retirement communities, with each club devising its own rules of play. The rules were finally formalized at St. Petersburg, Florida, in 1924.

Right: Ambassadors for the gridiron game, these U.S. Army players are playing at the White City Stadium, London, England in front of a mixed audience of British and Americans during World War II, May 22, 1943.

Far Left: Two American soldiers touching their boxing gloves together as they pose before their match in front of a barracks during the Civil War, c. 1865. Their seconds flank them on either side.

Left: Men and women climbers roped together on their way up to the summit of Mount Hood, Oregon, in 1913. Mount Hood is a dormant volcano and the highest mountain in Oregon at 11,237 ft. It has always been popular with climbers, skiers, and hikers. Its last major eruption was in the 1790s just before Lewis and Clark's expedition to the Pacific Northwest.

Below: Hot air balloons about to take off in this c. 1920 photograph. The name Gordon Bennett is clearly seen on two of the balloons. He was a wealthy Scottish-born American journalist who owned and published the *New York Herald* and who loved the new sport of ballooning. He is still associated with ballooning, as one of the sport's most important events still bears his name.

Left: "Babe" Ruth in action for the New York Yankees. Born George Herman Ruth on February 6, 1895, in Baltimore, Maryland, in 1914, at age nineteen, Ruth signed his first professional baseball contract for the Baltimore Orioles. Within five months he was sold to the Boston Red Sox and debuted as a major leaguer in Fenway Park on July 11, 1914, pitching against the Cleveland Indians. In December of 1919, Babe was sold to the Yankees. Photo dated April 9, 1925.

Above: Headgear has come a long way since the Roaring Twenties. Here American footballer "Hinkey" Haines of the New York Giants models the latest design of protective headgear, November 26, 1925.

Left: Two all-time great American heavyweight boxers—Jack Dempsey (1895–1983) and Gene Tunney (1897–1978), on September 20, 1926, before their first big fight. Dempsey was the World Heavyweight champion from 1919–26 and Tunney the challenger. Known as the "Manassa Mauler," Dempsey lost his title to Tunney and then lost the "Long Count" rematch in controversial circumstances. Dempsey knocked Tunney down in the seventh round but did not retire to a neutral corner immediately, so the referee delayed the count. Tunney got up at the count of nine and went on to win the bout. The count of nine was estimated to be a count of fourteen.

Right: Miss G. Schuyler, a member of an American women's lacrosse team, showing her determination to capture the ball. September 1935. Lacrosse is originally a Native American stick and ball game called *baggataway*, which means "little brother of war." French settlers named the game "la crosse" after the shape of the stick, which resembled a bishop's crozier.

Below: What it's really like inside the huddle, c. 1935.

Far Left: The outstanding athlete of his generation—Jesse James Cleveland Owens (1913–80) running at the 1936 Olympic Games in Germany where he won four gold medals—for the 100 meters, 200 meters, the long jump, and the 4 x 100 meters. Photograph taken in August 1936.

Left: Native American women of the Popago (bean-eating) tribal reserve in Sells, southern Arizona, playing a game of Taka, December 1950.

Below: The Brooklyn Dodgers baseball team in 1950.

Far Left: Goose Tatum of the Harlem Globetrotters basketball team which did so much to internationalize the game. Today played professionally all over the world, basketball came of age on the international stage in the Summer Olympics.

Left: Boxing Commissioner Bob Christenberry looks on as Sugar Ray Robinson and Joey Maxim sign the contracts for their fight at Yankee Stadium, May 12, 1956.

Below: Muhammad Ali, in training for his fight against the West German Jürgen Blin, takes his twin daughters out for a run, December 22, 1971. Undoubtedly the greatest heavyweight boxer ever, Ali brought a wit and skill to the ring that popularized the sport. He obviously influenced his daughters, too, as Laila Ali took to the ring and has done much to bring female boxing to the fore.

Above: Group portrait of a soccer team posing in front of a fence at the West Side Playground, 68th Street, New York City, c. 1895. While soccer has never been a major commercial sport in the United States, times are changing. The success of the 1994 World Cup, held in America, and the victory of the U.S. women's team in the 1998 World Cup seem to point to better times for soccer.

Right: Olympic swimming champion and later Hollywood actor Johnny Weissmuller, (1904–1984), the most popular screen Tarzan, December 26, 1934. United States teams have always enjoyed success in the Olympic swimming pool, with many outstanding talents. Possibly the greatest was Mark Spitz, who gained five golds in 1972, when he set, as one commentator put it, the pool alight with his talent.

Left: Sandskiers in Florida, June 6. 1964—an unusual but obviously enjoyable pastime.

ENTERTAINMENT

For people the world over, the entertainment industry is summed up in one word—Hollywood. It conjures all the glamor, excitement, and scandal of celebrity. Film, however, was a relatively late success story for an entertainment industry whose roots lay in traveling circuses, fairs, vaudeville, and local shows. Touring companies offering Shakespearean plays and melodramas took the stage to the country. They were eagerly-awaited events in far-flung towns, bringing with them a spot of culture and thespian allure. The circus or fair would come to town, pitch up in a field on the outskirts and send barkers into the streets to drum up customers, who would flock to the noise and excitement of the entertainments on show.

One of the most successful companies was Buffalo Bill's Wild West Show, started by William Frederick "Buffalo Bill" Cody. It started traveling around America in 1883 and proved so popular that the troupe toured abroad. The Wild West Show was a four-hour spectacular which purported to recreate—with genuine Native Americans and cowboys—all the romance of the Wild West. In 1887 the Wild West Show was performed at Madison Square Garden, New York City, with a cast of a hundred Native Americans, and included Annie Oakley (the celebrated sharpshooter, who had joined the company in 1885), trick riders, ropers, shooters, and even buffalo, elk, bear, moose, and deer. The show was a great attraction for over a decade during which it made millions, but by 1909 failing crowds and impending financial collapse (not helped by his poor business sense) forced Cody to sell out to his major rival, Pawnee Bill's Historic Far West and Great Far East Shows. However, even with united resources the crowds stayed away and the debts grew larger; the show went bankrupt and was forced to close in 1915.

From the 1860s until the 1920s, vaudeville was king. This offered a mixed variety of short variety skits including singing, comedians, magic acts, jugglers, and acrobats, all packaged together into an evening of fun and laughter. Such entertainments started just before the Civil War as rough and salacious free shows in concert saloons which were known as "free and easies" and Western "honky-tonks." The noisy and enthusiastic audience would be entirely male except for the prostitutes looking for business.

By the 1870s vaudeville had such a dreadful reputation that forward-looking entrepreneurs realized the shows needed cleaning-up to attract a better audience. The most successful at this was Tony

Right: A group of newsboys and shoeshine boys in caps playing craps on a sidewalk in front of a store, 1910.

Pastor, who opened his first vaudeville house in New York. He wanted to attract a much more family-oriented audience and to that effect banned the sale of intoxicating liquor and lewd performers and actively discouraged any audience rowdiness.

As a direct result of improving its image, vaudeville enjoyed its heyday between 1900 and 1925 when ten people went to vaudeville for every one who went to an alternative entertainment such as the theater. There was a huge national vaudeville circuit and a near-monopoly of acts and venues controlled by Keith and Albee. They imposed a rigid regime on performers and their salaries and brooked no dissent: they could afford to be particular, as there were between 10,000 and 20,000 vaudeville acts competing for bookings. The most popular stars were the best paid and could earn a very respectable fortune. The more far-sighted of them saw the end coming and moved off to the theater and to musical comedies; the luckiest managed to get into radio and then talking pictures,

which became the next audience-pleaser. By the end of the 1930s, vaudeville had disappeared altogether, replaced by the movies.

Novelty is often the key when it comes to entertainment and a new fad started in the 1890s—moving pictures. The kinetoscope, invented by Thomas Edison, presented flickering images of moving people and animals, and pictures of exotic places. The technology rapidly improved, and by 1901 every major city had a nickelodeon showing motion pictures. By 1914 Hollywood had become the home of the movies, supplanting New York, and a staggering three million people were going to the movies every day. Filmmaking, within a few short years, had become a giant money-making business, employing thousands and entertaining millions. The advent of television may have had a major effect on movie audiences, but it also stimulated filmmaking, and today film and television dominate the entertainment industry.

Left: The vaudeville musical duo Hartman and Rule, from Boulder Creek, Colorado, performing on stage in Chicago, c. 1915. She accompanies him on an accordion while he sings and plays the violin.

Above: Rosetta Duncan, the vaudeville performer (at left), and her sister Vivian Duncan resting during the filming of *Topsy and Eva*, based on *Uncle Tom's Cabin.*

Above: Henry Fonda on the set of *Grapes of Wrath* (he is on the cab roof) in the role of Tom Judd for which he won an Academy Award. The film was directed by John Ford and produced by 20th Century Fox.

Far Left: Surrounded by chorus girls, Jack Oakie (real name: Lewis Delaney Offield), an American comic actor who started his career in vaudeville. The blond girl on his left is Toby Wing, at the time labeled as Hollywood's prettiest chorus girl, c. 1935.

Left: Dancing inside the recreation tent of the Farm Security Administration agricultural workers' camp, Bridgetown, New Jersey, June 1942.

Right: A group of teenagers standing by a jukebox in a dance hall in Richwood, West Virginia, September 1942. For three decades after World War II, the jukebox enjoyed its heyday. The business was dominated by companies such as Rock-Ola—named after Canadian founder David C. Rockola, and Wurlitzer, whose founder, Rudolph, came to the United States in 1853 from Saxony. He attached a coin slot to a player piano and literally started the coin-operated music boom of the late 1800s. He also became famous for the large theater organs that created sound for silent films. The depression of 1929 nearly put the company out of business. In 1933, Rudolph's youngest son, Farny, entered into a deal to manufacture a coin phonograph called the "Debutante." The demand for coin-operated music was about to explode, and when it did, Wurlitzer collected. By 1937 the company had sold over 100,000 phonographs. Wurlitzer dominated the coin-operated phonograph business until the introduction of the 45-rpm record. At that point, Wurliter's mechanism could handle up to twenty-four records, playing only one side. Swedish company J. P. Seeburg originally produced automatic pianos. Seeburg's son Noel was in charge when the company introduced a new mechanism that held fifty records and could play both sides, yielding a true 100-selection jukebox. This ensured that by the 1950s Seeburg was the predominant jukebox manufacturer. It would hold this claim until the 1970s when the jukebox business collapsed.

Top: A large group of senior citizens playing cards on a summer afternoon at a park off Paul Reeves Mall, Boston, Massachusetts. A war memorial is mounted on the wall behind them, c. 1955.

Above: Gamblers play craps in Las Vegas, Nevada, one of the few areas in the country to legalize gambling. November 6, 1965.

Left: Guests at a fancy dress party show all of Hollywood's renowned restraint! This 1950 photograph was taken at the Romanoff Restaurant in Hollywood, c. 1950.

HUNTING, FISHING, & SHOOTING

Hunting, fishing, and shooting are true all-American pursuits. In the earliest days they were a necessity to fill the pot or protect livestock; today they are mainly sports.

Native Americans traditionally hunted buffalo for all their living requirements—their flesh for food, their hides for clothing and covering their tepees, and their bones and sinews for tools. It was obvious to the settlers who coveted Native American tribal lands that by hunting the buffalo to extinction they would rapidly hasten the demise of the native tribes and would, therefore, be able to take their lands with minimal resistance.

In 1850 there were an estimated sixty million buffalo roaming the lands, only lightly culled by the native tribes as their needs required. The authorities, in the form of the state governments, encouraged the hunting of the buffalo herds, ostensibly for food, but actually to eliminate native and local opposition to settler expansion. In the 1870s as the railroads were built, the buffalo were ruthlessly taken to feed the work crews; in 1871 alone, over four million buffalo were killed, and by 1883 there were only a few hundred buffalo left. Their numbers have never recovered to anything like their former glory.

Hunting is inextricably linked to guns, the private ownership of which and right to bear them in the United States was sanctioned in 1791 by the Second Amendment to the Constitution. This declares that "A well-regulated militia being necessary to the security of a free State, the right of the people to keep and bear arms shall not be infringed." Because of this, gun control has always been contentious, and the hunting lobby is just one section of the public that defends its right to bear arms with determination.

Each time an important national figure is assassinated—such as John F. Kennedy or Martin Luther King, Jr.—or an outrageous gun crime is committed, the issue is raised again, alongside its inevitable relationship with violent crime. Despite this, the National Rifle Association actively campaigns against controls on the purchase and possession of guns—even weapons obviously designed for military use—as an unwarranted restraint on personal liberty.

The numbers of guns in private ownership rose alarmingly in the twentieth century, as increasing numbers were manufactured, and

Right: Two sportsmen camp in a forest clearing. One man, wearing hip waders, drinks from a mug next to their tent while the other kneels by a fire to prepare breakfast. Fishing rods lean against their tent, c. 1965.

Above: Proud anglers with their catch of sailfish, c.1925.

Left: A man holds a massive lobster caught at Provincetown in Cape Cod, c. 1925. It was 3 ft., 6 in. long, weighed twenty-seven pounds, and was said to be fifty years old.

veterans from both World Wars and other conflicts smuggled home their personal weapons and any others they could find. A conservative estimate in the 1990s put the number of guns in the United States at 66 million and rising.

For both hunting and fishing, the laws have historically changed over time and across regions according to the population of the hunted species. The seasonal dates for hunting and trapping are revised annually, and licenses and special permits have to be obtained before any hunting can be commenced. This measure does not control illegal hunting and

trapping, but does prevail over the honest majority of sportsmen, allowing stocks of their prey to rebuild.

Since the mid-1960s a greater sense of the environment and the importance of protecting flora and fauna has governed much of the licensing for fishing and hunting. In years when the population of a species is low, it can be that hunting of that particular species is banned altogether. The number—as well as age, size, and weight—of animals caught is strictly regulated, particularly in the case of pregnant animals and their young.

Fishing is a national passion and one of the most popular hobbies in the United States. America is a rich land for both freshwater and saltwater fishing. For example, in New York State there are over forty-five different species of fish to catch in the literally thousands of lakes and ponds, not to mention rivers and streams across the state. The Caribbean is the cradle of big-game sports fishing, and from the quays of Florida and the Gulf, many sportsmen pit their strength and guile against that of their adversaries—shark, swordfish, and marlin.

Above: An Inuit woman and her daughter fish through a hole on an icy expanse in Alaska, c. 1950.

Left: Three young women with their fishing rods head off for an angling trip, February 1941.

Far Left: Wolf hunters in Minnesota advance with bows ready. Wolves and snowshoe rabbits are their only quarry in the wildlife sanctuary of the University of Minnesota. The severe reduction in wolf numbers caused by hunting led to a reassessment of this much-maligned animal. Today, thanks to conservation and breeding programs, some wolves are being reintroduced into the wild, although to a mixed response by local farmers. Photograph taken c. 1950.

Left: A hunter sitting on the carcass of a whale he has just caught in Alaska, c. 1955. Another animal that has benefited from conservation and fishing quotas, today whales in Alaskan waters are more likely to be chased by tourists or cameramen from television programs.

Above: Robert Bridge, a snake hunter in Reptile Jungle, Slidell, Louisiana, fishing for a cottonmouth or water mocassin snake, c. 1956.

Left: A crocodile being carried through the swamps by hunters in Reptile Jungle, Slidell, Louisana, c. 1956.

VACATIONS & FESTIVALS

Until recently, vacations were the province of the wealthy. Some workers could enjoy the occasional holiday, and possibly even travel by rail or bicycle, but it wasn't until the advent of the cheap, private motor car that people could travel far enough and quickly enough to vacation anywhere other than at home or close by. In the 1920s, for the first time anybody with an automobile had the freedom to travel wherever they wanted, whenever they wanted—and consequently the vacation business was born

As industrialization spread across America, so working conditions changed to allow for more sociable working hours. Organized labor and lobbyists pleaded with Congress to improve the lot of the working man, and slowly, things improved. In 1860 an ordinary citizen worked on average for some sixty-six hours a week; by 1914 this had been reduced to fifty-five hours. Nevertheless, it took a long time for the reduction in working hours to become real leisure time, or for consecutive days to be taken as free time. When it did, the vacation arrived.

With time and personal mobility available, suddenly the nation began to travel. Motels and wayside restaurants sprang up to service these new travelers, serving drinks, ice cream, hot meals, gas, and sundry items such as newspapers and magazines. For the first time, poor people could enjoy the freedom of traveling the roads with relatively little expense—gas was cheap to buy and so were cars.

However, it was after World War II that the vacation business really took off. The arrival of cheap air travel made the continent shrink. Soon, Americans could vacation in the sun—in Florida or on the West Coast—visit the Caribbean islands, or for the adventurous few, cross the Atlantic to look at the Old World. As leisure time became a business, there were other changes as well. One of the greatest changes was the development of the theme park—an entertainment complex designed to cater to vacationers and their families. The best-known of these is Disneyland in California, created by Walt Disney as an adjunct to his film studio. After much searching

Right: Young girls holding the U.S. and British flags while sitting in a forest clearing with a counselor at a summer camp. They are wearing their hair braided on either side with headbands in the tradition of Native Americans, c. 1910.

Left: A group of American Youth Hostel members on a cycling trip through the countryside around Minneapolis, Minnesota, c. 1950. The 1950s were a great time for Americans. The country had never before enjoyed such good economic times: between 1946 and 1956 national output doubled and sixty percent of Americans saw increased earnings and leisure time. The youth of the day benefited enormously, with summer camps and other facilities available.

Far Left: Workmen inflating a giant 45-foot Santa Claus with helium on November 21, 1940, for the Macy's Parade, New York. This annual procession is held every Thanksgiving for Macy's department store. While many people in the United States will take a summer vacation, Thanksgiving is always a good reason for families to travel.

for suitable real estate on which to build his dream world, Disney bought a 160-acre orange grove near rural Anaheim, California, with the intention of opening to the paying public in the summer of 1955. Construction on the site started on July 21, 1954, and the orange trees were cleared and fifteen houses demolished. Walt Disney himself oversaw almost every detail of the project, which cost $17 million, a huge sum at the time. The opening day was a disaster, with thousands of curious customers turning up clutching counterfeit tickets, and California was in the middle of a 110°F heat wave which melted the tarmac. The continuing heat wave almost destroyed the theme park, but eventually the crowds came. By 1965, Disneyland could claim that fifty million visitors had passed though its gates. By the end of the century, it had been replicated at Disney World in Florida and at Disneyland Paris in France—and had spawned thousands of imitators worldwide.

Left: Jewish children celebrating the spring festival of Purim (Lots), c. 1950. Mass immigration and religious tolerance have led to myriad festivals in the United States. One of the most colorful and lively is the Irish St. Patrick's Day celebration that has become almost a national institution with rivers dyed green and major parades in large cities, particularly New York.

Far Left: A young woman shaking a blossom tree branch over a friend by a swimming pool at Sun Valley, a skiing resort in Idaho, c. 1950.

Below: Easter has always been an important festival and holiday for Christians. These are crowds on Fifth Avenue, New York on Easter Day, 1950.

Left: City children playing at being farmers while vacationing on a Long Island farm, c. 1956.

Far Left: One of the highlights of the winter—walking through the snow to collect the family Christmas tree, December 1955.

Below: Piles of pumpkins in a New York street market, on sale for Halloween celebrations in 1975.

Above: Showgirls at the Vermont state fair in Rutland, Vermont, September 1941.

Right: Miss Victory, Eglie Zacchini, being fired out of a cannon at the New York Circus, June 28, 1943.

Far Right: A floating celebration of the life of John Audubon (1785–1851), the American naturalist, ornithologist, and artist at the New Orleans Mardi Gras in Louisiana in 1956. The official colors of Mardi Gras—gold, purple, and green—are used to decorate the revelers, the floats, and the streets.

ACKNOWLEDGMENTS

The photograph of Solomon D Butcher
that appears at the top left hand corner
of page 16, and at the start of chapters
throughout the book, appears by kind per-
mission of the Nebraska State Historical
Society [Digital ID: nbhips 16311].

The photograph of the American flag that
appears at the top left hand corner of
page 16, and at the start of chapters
throughout the book, was taken by Simon
Clay.

The photograph on page 116-117 (main)
was supplied by Chrysalis Images.

The publisher wishes to thank
Hulton|Archive for kindly supplying all the
other photography in this book, including
the cover photography, with additional
credits as follows:

George Eastman House/Lewis W.
Hine/Hulton|Archive for front cover and
    pages 158-159, 176-177 (main),
    219, 238 (bottom), 320-321
    (main), 332 (bottom), 333, 340
    (top), 352-353, 354 (left) and
    406-407 (main);
John Margolies/Hulton|Archive for pages
    12 and 276 (top);
Library of Congress/Hulton|Archive for
    pages 36 (bottom), 238 (top), 243
    (top), 246-247 (main), 255 (bot
    tom), 276 (bottom), 277, 286,
    287 (top left), 287 (top right), 288
    (top), 319 (top), 354 (right), 355,
    356 (top left), 358 (bottom), 368-
    369, 370, 389 (top), 389 (bot
    tom), 412, 440 (bottom left) and

442 (top);
George Eastman House/Samuel N.
    Fox/Hulton|Archive for pages 37
    (top right);
Hirz/Hulton|Archive for pages 74-75
    (main), 260 (bottom) and 294-295
    (main);
American Stock/Hulton|Archive for pages
    88 (top), 265, 316-317 (main)
    and 378 (bottom);
Slim Aarons/Hulton|Archive for pages 88
    (bottom), 268 (top), 313 (bottom)
    and 414-415 (main);
Museum of the City of New York/Byron
    Collection/Hulton|Archive for
    pages 129 (top), 130 (bottom),
    207, 216 (bottom), 256-257
    (main), 259 (top), 274-275 (top)
    and 332 (top);
New York Times Co./Hulton|Archive for
    page 154 (top);
George Eastman House/Victor
    Keppler/Hulton|Archive for page
    154 (bottom) and 264 (top);
George Eastman House/B.F.
    Childs/Hulton|Archive for page
    217 (top);
Lambert/Hulton|Archive for pages 220-
    221 (main), 236 (top), 337 (bot
    tom), 380 (top left) and 416-417
    (main);
CBS Photo Archive/Hulton|Archive for
    page 223;
NASA/Hulton|Archive for 227 (top);
Museum of the City of New York/Jacob A.
    Riis/Hulton|Archive for pages 240
    (left) and 404 (top);
George Eastman House/Alfred
    Stieglitz/Hulton|Archive for page
    258 (bottom);
John Kobal Foundation/Hulton|Archive for
    pages 260 (top) and 405;
Archive Photos/Hulton|Archive for pages
    262 (top left), 262 (bottom left),
    262-263 (main), 264 (bottom),
    306-307 (main), 310 (bottom),
    341 and 380-381 (main);
Edwin Levick/Hulton|Archive for page 275
    (bottom);
International Centre of Photography for
    pages 289, 401 (bottom), 428
    and 442 (bottom);
George Enell/Hulton|Archive for pages
    390-391;
George Eastman House/Hulton|Archive
    for page 394 (top);
Scott Swanson Collection/Hulton|Archive
    for pages 408 and 426-427
    (main);
Anthony Potter Collection/Hulton|Archive
    for page 411 (bottom).